Contents

COMMUNICATION AND EDUCATION TECHNOLOGY FOR NURSES BSC 2ND YEAR NURSING

PREVIOUS YEAR CHAPTER WISE SOLVED QUESTION AND ANSWERS.

RUTWIK UPENDRA BHALSHANKAR

CHAPTER ONE

COMMUNICATION

SHORT ANSWER QUESTIONS

Q 1. Define communication .

= **Communication is the process of sending and receiving messages between parties .**

Defination :

Webster's New Collegiate dictionary defines communication as a process by which information is exchanged between individuals through a common system of symbols, signs or behavior .

Communication is interchange of thoughts, opinions or information by speech, writing or signs.

—Robert Anderson

To some communication is the exchange of information between two or more people, in other sense the exchange of ideas or thought.

Q 2. What is communication process? / . Write down the elements of communication process.

= communication as a process by which information is exchanged between individuals through a common system of symbols, signs or behavior .

Communication is interchange of thoughts, opinions or information by speech, writing or signs.

The communication process through seven steps. They are:

Source or sender: The person or objects which passes information or ideas to other persons is known as sender or source

Ideas: This is the subject matter of communication. This might be opinions, attitudes, feelings, views, suggestions, orders etc.

Encoding: Conversion of subject matter into symbols (words, actions, pictures etc.) is the process of encoding. Symbols are transmitted from the sender to the receiver.

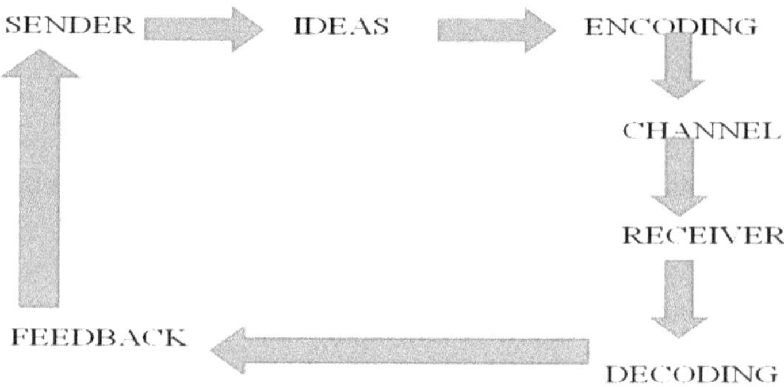

communication process

Channel: The symbols are transmitted through certain channels, e.g. radio, telephone, speech, written message, gestures etc. depending upon the relative distance between the sender and the receiver

Receiver: Receiver is the person to whom the message is meant for

Decoding: Receiver converts the symbol received from the sender to give him the meaning of the message

Feedback: Feedback is the response from the receiver. Feedback is necessary to ensure that the receiver has received the message and understood it in the same sense as sender wants.

Q 3. Write down the channels of communication process.

= communication as a process by which information is exchanged between individuals through a common system of symbols, signs or behavior .

Communication is interchange of thoughts, opinions or information by speech, writing or signs.

Channel :

A channel is a medium through which a message is sent or received between two or more people. Several channels can be used to send or receive the message, i.e. seeing, hearing, touching, smelling and tasting.

It is believed that when a sender uses more than one channel, the message is delivered more effectively and communication is smoother. For example, when teaching a patient about the use of incentive spirometry, the patient will understand more easily if a nurse uses conversation along with the demonstration of techniques.

Types of channels

Visual channels: Visual channels of communication are considered to be the most primitive because they have been used since before languages were developed. They are primarily used to send messages through nonverbal communication. Some of the nonverbal channels are facial expressions, body language, posture, gestures, pictures, written symbols, words, etc. Nurses are commonly found using visual channels to send or receive messages to their patients or health care team. For example, when a nurse in a medical unit observes a patient sleeping in an awkward position and repeatedly touching his or her abdomen, the nurse receives a message (through visual channels) that the patient is not comfortable and may be experiencing pain or discomfort in the abdomen. In another instance, when a scrubbed nurse involved in assisting with a surgical procedure needs gauze pieces, she asks the circulatory nurse to supply them by showing her four fingers indicating the number of gauzes to be supplied. In large organizations, most communication is carried out by written circulars, memos, e-mails, personal letters and notices. However, visual channels of communication are used most frequently and promptly in the general as well as health care scenario.

Channels	Types of Message
1. Visual	Facial expressions, body language, posture, gestures, pictures and written words, electronic mails, mass media, etc.
2. Auditory	Spoken words, sounds, telephone or mobile communications, delivering audio content (radio, voicemail), etc.
3. Tactile	Touch sensations, therapeutic touch, etc.
4. Combined	Audiovisual media, consoling a person with touch and spoken words.

Channels of communication process

- **Auditory channels :**

Auditory channels are used to send or receive verbal communication messages. Auditory channels are the most frequently used channels of communication and involve using spoken words and sounds to transmit messages between two or more individuals. Auditory channels are the cheapest, easiest, quickest and universally available channels of communication. For example, when nurses want to collect the health-illness history from patients and their families, they prefer to use auditory channels of communication so they can promptly, easily and cost-effectively communicate with the patients and their family.

- **Tactile channels**: Tactile channels involve conveying messages through touch. For example, nurses wanting to show sympathy towards a patient in grief and loss will use touch to show their concern. This channel of communication is less frequently used, but is considered one of the most powerful of channels for conveying emotions.

- **Combined channels:** As the name suggests, these are the use of more than one channels of communication at any given instance to send or receive messages. It is widely believed and proven by research that the use of combined channels of communication is a stronger means for effective communication.

Q 4. Importance's of communication .

= communication as a process by which information is exchanged between individuals through a common system of symbols, signs or behavior .

Communication is interchange of thoughts, opinions or information by speech, writing or signs.

- Clear and appropriate communication is essential for maintaining good interpersonal relationships and providing effective nursing care.
- Overcoming barriers to communication is necessary where the population is multicultural.
- Non- verbal communication has different meanings in the different cultures
- Clear communication about client & his care is important
- Provides better resources to the
- profession
- Means of personal and social interaction between the people.
- It is a basic component of human relationships
- Nurses who communicate effectively are better able to:-
- Initiate change that promotes health
- Establish a trusting relationship with the client and support persons
- Prevent legal problems associated with nursing practice (Negligence,Malpractice)
- It is essential in interdisciplinary teams

Q 5. Discuss the characteristics to facilitate effective communication.

= communication as a process by which information is exchanged between individuals through a common system of symbols, signs or behavior .

Communication is interchange of thoughts, opinions or information by speech, writing or signs.

characteristics to facilitate effective communication.

- Have a positive attitude about communication.
- Defensiveness interferes with communication.
- Work at improving communication skills.
- Increased awareness for improving communication is the first step to better communication.
- Include communication as a skill to be evaluated along with all other skill.
- Help other people to improve their communication skills by helping them to understand their communication problems.
- Make communication goal oriented.
- Approach communication as a creative process rather than simply part of working with people.
- Accept the reality of miscommunication.
- Warmth and friendliness maintains the quality of communication.
- Openness and respect- an attitude of acceptance,
- Empathy, identifying with the way another person feels.
- Comfortable environment helps to create the trustable and safe environment for communication

Q 6.. Enlist the barriers to communication.

= communication as a process by which information is exchanged between individuals through a common system of symbols, signs or behavior .

Communication is interchange of thoughts, opinions or information by speech, writing or signs.

- **Physical Barriers:** Physical distraction is the physical things that get in the way of communication. E.g. telephone, desk, uncomfortable meeting place, closed office doors, barrier screens etc.
    - Poor Health, Fatigue, hearing Defect, Speech Defect
- **Perceptual Barriers:** The problem with communicating with others is that we all see the world differently. Something like extra sensory perception would take place.
- **Emotional Barriers:** One of the chief barrier comprised mainly of fear, worry, anxiety, etc.
- **Cultural Barriers:** Every culture has their own symbol of behaviour. If these symbols are not understood by an individual then there is barrier in their communication.
- **Language barriers:**Language is vehicle for communication which describes what we want to say. It presents barriers to others who are not familiar with our expressions, buzz words and jargon.
- **Gender Barriers:** There are distinct differences between the speech patterns in a man and in woman.
    - Man talks in a linear, logical and compartmentalized way and features of left brain thinking, whereas a woman talks more freely mixing logic, emotions and features of both sides of the brain.
- **Interpersonal Barriers:**
    - There are some levels at which people can distance themselves from one another.

- **Withdrawal** – is van absence of interpersonal contact. It is both refusal to be in touch and time alone.
- **Rituals** – are meaningless, repetitive routines devoid of routine contacts.
- **Past Time** – fill up time with others in social but superficial activities.
- **Working**- activities are those tasks which follows the rules and procedures of contact.
- **Closeness**- the aim of interpersonal contact where there is a high level of honesty and acceptance of self and others.

- **Wrong channel:**channels help the receiver to understand the nature and importance of the message. "Good morning" an oral channel is highly appropriate than writing it on a board.
- **Lack of feedback:** feedback is the mirror of the communication.
- .**Intellectual:** Level of understanding, Lack of knowledge, Low IQ, Misinterpretation of words
- **Social:**Cultural differences, languages .

Q 7 Enlist the techniques of communication.

= communication as a process by which information is exchanged between individuals through a common system of symbols, signs or behavior .

Communication is interchange of thoughts, opinions or information by speech, writing or signs.

Techniques of effective communication:

Conversation skills:

a. It is social interaction.
n. Control the tone of the voice so that you convey exactly what you mean to say and not a hidden message.
n. Be knowledgeable about the topic of conversation and have accurate information.

n. Be flexible, clear and concise.
n. Avoid words that may be interpreted differently.
n. Keep an open mind.
n. Take advantage of available opportunity.

n. **Listening skills**: Involves both hearing and interpreting.

n. It requires attention and concentration to sort out, evaluate and validate clues in order to better understanding the true meaning of what is being said.
n. Whenever possible sit with person, do not cross your arms or legs because that body language conveys a message of being closed.
n. Be alert but relaxed and take sufficient time so that the patient feels at ease during the conversation..
n. Keep the conversation as natural as possible & avoid so overly eager
n. If culturally appropriate maintain eye contact with the person. Indicate your attention by using appropriate facial expressions and body gesture.
n. Think before feedback.

Q 8 . Write the qualities of a good communicator .

= **The Qualities of a Good communicator :**
Respect and empathy for the client .Good communication skills .Tolerance of values and beliefs different from one's own .Unbiased attitudes .Patience .Awareness of gender issues.

- Be authentic, honest, and open.
- Be engaging, interesting, and approachable.
- Listen actively, attentively, and with understanding.
- Use appropriate body language and facial expressions, maintain good eye contact, and show empathy.

Here are six qualities that all good communicators have in common that you can use to both train those around you and improve your own abilities:

- They are honest. In the short-term, it can be easier to be untruthful. ...
- They are proactive. ...
- They ask **good** questions. ...
- They listen. ...
- They are concise. ...
- They are reliable.

CHAPTER TWO

INTERPERSONAL RELATION

SHORT ANSWER QUESTIONS

Q 1. Define Interpersonal relationship.

a. = Interpersonal Relationships are social association, connections or affiliation between two or more people.

n. It is a long term association and it is based on emotions like love and liking, regular business interactions etc.

n. These relationships can be seen in family, friends, marriage, in neighborhood, churches etc.

Definition

n. Interpersonal Relationship refers to reciprocal social and emotional interaction between two or more individuals in an environment.

n. Interpersonal Relationship is defined as a close association between individuals who share common interest and goals.

Q 2. Barriers of Interpersonal relations.

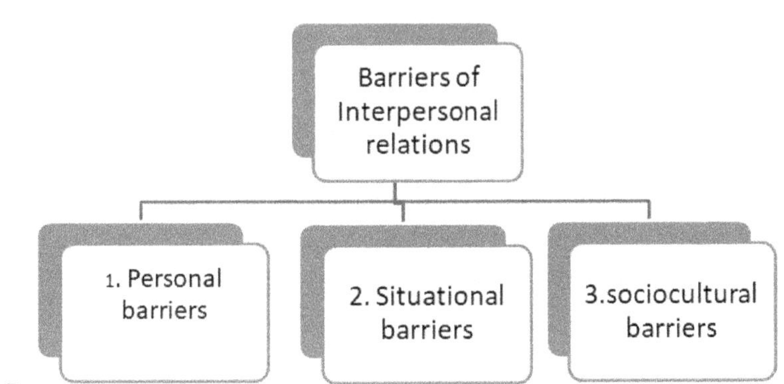

Barriers of Interpersonal relations.

1. **Personal barriers**

The major personal factors that can influence the development or maintenance of an interpersonal relationship between two or more people are discussed below.

- **Gender:** Gender may influence an interpersonal relationship. A strange man may establish a prompt and intimate interpersonal relation with another man. However, the same may not ensue between a man and a woman and vice versa.
- **Lack of honesty and trust:** Absence of honesty and trust between two or more individuals may affect their interpersonal relationships. Therefore, the presence of honesty and trust are essential factors in the development of interpersonal relationships. In the absence of honesty, an inner positive feeling of closeness may not be established and trust cannot be built, which is one of the fundamental prerequisites for building strong interpersonal relationships.
- **Lack of compatibility:** Reciprocal compatibility is essential for a strong interpersonal relationship. Two individuals with a

contrasting personality, who are not at all compatible, may face difficulties in getting along with each other and may not be able to establish a good interpersonal relationship.

- **Feelings of insecurity:** When individuals lack security in a relationship, they may fail to establish a good interpersonal relationship because of feelings of threat and anxiety that may hinder a strong interpersonal relationship.

Lack of integrity

- Arrogance
- Manipulative behaviour
- Closed mind
- Inconsistency
- Suspiciousness
- Past bad experiences
- Lack of discipline
- Lack of courtesy
- Impatience
- Not meeting commitments
- Selfishness

II. Situational barriers

Situational barriers play a major role in interpersonal relationship as well. Some major situational factors that influence interpersonal relationships are discussed below.

Adverse environmental situations:

Environment is where the transition takes place. It can be a problem to maintain an interpersonal relationship if the environment is not cordial. Adverse environmental situations always play a crucial role in blocking interpersonal relationships.

- **Lack of territoriality**: Territoriality is the innate tendency to own space. All individuals lay claim to certain areas as their own and feel safer in their own area. Lack of territoriality leads to distortion in interpersonal relationships.

- **High density of individuals:** Density refers to the number of people within a given environmental space. Prolonged exposure to high-density situations elicits certain behaviours, such as aggression, stress and hostility. These behaviours can stop a person from building effective interpersonal relationships.
- **Increased physical distance:** The means by which various cultures use space to communicate. If this distance is more than required, sometimes it can be a source of hindrance in interpersonal relationships. There are certain specifications about the distance to be kept in interpersonal relationships (e.g. intimate distance: the closest distance individuals allow between themselves and others is recommended at being about 0–18 inches .
- **Lack of time**: Time plays an important role in relationships. Every relationship needs time and an individual's effort to grow. Frustrations arise when people do not have time to meet or interact with each other. Even in organizations, individuals must spend quality time with their co-workers to strengthen the bond between them. Married couples must take time out for each other for the magic to stay in the relationship forever.

III. Sociocultural barriers

Some common sociocultural barriers of interpersonal relationships are given below.

- **Cultural diversity:** Culture plays an important role in the development of interpersonal relationships as cultural mores, norms, ideas and customs provide the basis for our way of thinking. For example, a man and a woman who hug each other on the street give a different message in the Indian culture than they would in the American culture. Similarly, an organization's culture (which can be a hospital setting also) influences the general nature of employee relationships.

Q 3 .Explain the methods of overcoming the barriers in IPR.

= Methods to overcome barriers of interpersonal relationships Several strategies or guidelines may be used to overcome the barriers of interpersonal relationships. The essential guidelines to overcome these barriers are given below and in.

I . Strategies to overcome personal barriers

• In interpersonal relationships, gender differences must be given due consideration

. • Honesty and trust must be maintained while establishing and building interpersonal relationships.

• Individuals involved in an interpersonal relationship must be compatible.

• Individuals must try and adapt according to the others' backgrounds and try to be compatible with their aims, attitudes and thought processes.

• A sense of security must be ensured between the people involved in an interpersonal relationship.

• Effective communication is a key aspect of efficient interpersonal relationships. Clarity of thought is also essential in interpersonal relationships.

• Individuals involved in an interpersonal relationship must have a sound self-concept and positive self-esteem

. • Individuals must try and improve self-concept by minimizing the use of misperception and selective interaction and evaluation of the other person. They must also avoid selective self-evaluation and response evocation.

• Flexibility in ideology and philosophy of the individuals in a relationship must be ensured for a more effective adaptation and the success of an interpersonal relationship.

• A mutual sense of respect must be ensured by the people involved in a personal and professional relationship. • Fear of rejection must be eliminated between the individuals involved in an interpersonal relationship. • Skilled therapeutic communication is required to interact with individuals suffering from psychiatric or personality problems.

II. Strategies to overcome situational barriers

• The interaction setting should be simple and familiar to the individuals and each individual should make the other feel as important.

• During interaction in adverse environmental situations or between individuals of diverse territories and high densities, special care must be taken.

• Even in organizations, individuals must spend quality time with their co-workers to strengthen the bond between them.

III. Strategies to overcome sociocultural barriers

• One can try to overcome the cultural diversity by trying to enhance the four primary factors that decide the interaction pattern such as openness, trust, owing and risk to experiment.

• **In situations** of social diversity between the people involved in a relationship, individuals should try to understand their social variations and make a sincere effort to adapt to these variations with flexibility.

• Individuals must try to enhance interpersonal communication skills such as maintaining good eye contact, appropriate body language and listening with patience.

Steps to overcomeBarriers in Interpersonal Relationship

Steps 1 –

n. Admit that you have problem in relationship.
n. Identify the symptoms of the problem.
n. Write down the problem.
n. Then write, how you know if it is a problem by listing symptom present in your relationship.

Steps 2 –

n. Based on your admission in step 1 of the problem in your relationship, decide which of the barriers listed are present in this problem. List down that.

Steps 3 -

n. Once you have listed the problem and symptoms in step 1 and the barriers in step 2, share this list with your partner/ friends/ Colleagues to read your description in step 1 and step 2.

Steps 4 -

n. Based and your partner / friends/Colleagues responses in step 3, you both can compare your responses to the three questions. You are ready for an analysis of your different and similar points of view.
n. Write down on which points you agree or disagree concerning the problem, its symptoms and the barriers present.

Steps 5 –

n. you and your partner / friends/Colleagues are ready to develop a plan of action to address those barriers (problems) you agree exist in your specific relationship.

Q 4 . Importance of interpersonal relationship in nursing .

= The ability to communicate effectively is one of the most essential skills in nursing.

Communication encompasses (cause) study of the patient's behavior including all observable actions, verbal and non-verbal communication.

Effective communication goes beyond the nurse-patient relationship and involves co-ordination and co-operation with all of the health team members.

Nurse's responsibility in maintaining Interpersonal Relationship:

- Initiate the relationship by introducing herself.
- State the purpose of the relationship
- State the limitations of the relationship, including the frequency of interaction, duration and nature of the relationship.
- Maintain client – centered, pursuing mutually identified goals and exploring appropriate feelings of the patient.
- Terminate the relationship by preparing herself and the client for termination prior to the time for it, summarizing the relationship with the patient.
- Encourage the client to verbalize feelings about relationship, termination and expressing her own thoughts to the patient about the relationship.
- Like any powerful agent, the nurse's communication can result in both bad and good.
- Every nuance of posture, small expression, gesture, word chosen and attitude held have the potential to hurt or heal.
- Good communication empowers and enables people to know themselves and make their own choices.
- Nurses have good opportunities to bring about good things for themselves, their clients and their colleagues through the kind of therapeutic communication.

Nurse patient relationship:

Helping relationships are the foundation of clinical nursing practice.

In such relationship, nurse assumes the role of professional helper and comes to know the patient as an individual who has unique health needs, human responses and patterns of living.

Q 5. Johari window .

=The Johari window model is a simple and useful tool for illustrating and improving self-awareness and mutual understanding between individuals within a group.

The Johari window terminology refers to self and others. Self refers to the person subject to the Johari window analysis and others refers to other people in the person's group or team.

It is a simple and useful tool for understanding and training :-

- Self awareness
- Personal development
- Improving communication
- Interpersonal relationship
- Group dynamics
- Team development
- Inter group relationship

II. The concept of johari window

The word window in the Johari window model represents an open area or quadrant of one's personality (similar to a window in a house through which one can look inside or outside) which actually represents information especially feelings, views, attitudes, intentions, skills, etc., within or about a person from four different perspectives.

These perspectives are also known as regions, areas or quadrants. Thus, the Johari window model can be referred to as a disclosure/feedback model of self-awareness because it helps a person analyze his or her feelings or behavior and is an information processing tool for other people because they can process information about a person subjected to the Johari window analysis. Therefore, the terminology used in this model refers to self and others: self means oneself or a future group and others means other people in the person's group or other future groups who are subjected to the Johari window analysis.

The Johari window's four regions (areas, quadrants or perspectives) are as follows (Fig.

	Known to self	Not known to self
Known to others	Open	Blind
Not known to others	Hidden	Unknown

Johari window

1.Open area/open self/free area/free self: This is the part of an individual's personality that is open for the individual himself or herself and for others also. It represents all that is known by the person about himself or herself and is also known by others.

this area related to the information pertaining to behaviors, attitudes, experiences, motivation, emotions, feelings that is known to the self & by others.

2. Blind area/blind self/blind spot: As the quadrant's name implies, this is the area of one's personality about which the individual is totally unaware, i.e. the person does not know about his or her behavior or feelings but other people are aware about those.

this can be the simple information of deep issue such as incompetence, inadequacy, rejection, unworthiness which are difficult for individual to face directly & yet can be seen by others.

3. **Hidden area/hidden self/avoided area/avoided self:** This is the area that includes feelings, fears, etc., that are known to the person about himself or herself but are purposely hidden from others because of some reasons. Represents information, feelings, emotions known to self but not revealed to others.

Includes sensitiveness, secrets, fears, hidden agendas, manipulative intensions that a person doesn't want to reveal.

4. Unknown area/unknown self: This is the area that is not known to the person about himself or herself and others also do not know about the person.

Nurses can help in prompting through self-discovery or observations by others, or through collective or mutual discovery. Counseling can also uncover unknown issues.

These areas include repressed or Subconscious feelings rooted in formative events and traumatic past experiences, which can stay unknown for lifetime.

CHAPTER THREE

HUMAN RELATION

SHORT ANSWER QUESTIONS

Q 1. What do you understand by Self-understanding?

= Definitions of understanding self

Understanding self represents the sum total of people's conscious perception of their identity as distinct from others. It is not a static phenomenon, but continues to develop and change throughout our lives. — George Herbert Head

The understanding self is thinking about what is involved in being? What distinguish you from being an object, an animal or different person?

—Richard Stevens

Self understanding is **important** because when we have a better **understanding** of ourselves, we are able to experience ourselves as unique and separate individuals. We are then empowered to make changes and to build on our areas of strength as well as identify areas where we would like to make improvements.

Importance of understanding self

Self-understanding has been recognized as a key competency for individuals to function the organizations efficiently. It influences an individual's ability to make key decisions about self, others around and organizations. As a result, it influences our effectiveness in work, the directions taken in our lives and our degree of fulfilment.

Understanding the self equips individuals with making more effective career and life choices, the ability to strengthen relationships with others in their personal and professional life

and their ability to lead, guide and inspire with authenticity resulting in significantly improved organizational productivity. Self-understanding can be accomplished by assessing an individual's personality preference, interests, values, skills, conflict style, learning style, leadership style and life experiences.

PHYSICAL SELF IMAGE:- (Body image)

a. It is usually formed first and is related to the child's physical appearance, its attractiveness, sex appropriateness, the importance of the different body parts to behavior and to the percentage they give the child in eyes of other.
n. An individual body image is a personal appraisal of his or her physical being and includes physical attributes, functioning, sexuality, wellness- illness state and appearance. It is an integrated collection of visual, auditory, and tactile information that combines with effective and cognitive process to form image of one's physical self.

Psychological self-image:-

n. It is based on thoughts, feelings and emotions.
n. They consist of the qualities and abilities that affect adjustment to life such as courage, honesty, independence and self-confidence..

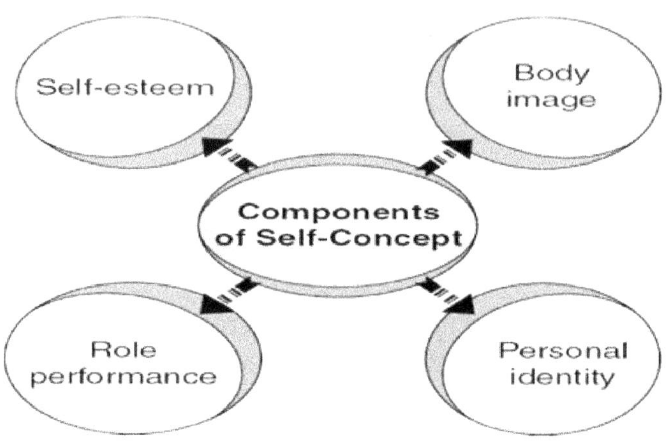

Self- esteem:-

n. It refers to the degree of regard or respect that individuals have for them and is a measure of worth that they place on their

abilities and judgment.

n. Self- esteem is closely related to the other components of the self respect.

PERSONAL BODY IMAGE :

n. An individual body image is a personal appraisal of his or her physical being and includes physical attributes, functioning, sexuality, wellness- illness state and appearance.
n. It is an integrated collection of visual, auditory, and tactile information that combines with effective and cognitive process to form image of one's physical self.

Q 2. Social behavior

= **Social behavior**

The interaction between members of the same species or the behavior directed towards the society is known as social behavior.

Communication between members of two different species is not social behavior.

It is an activity that has a social meaning or context. In a sociological hierarchy, social behavior is followed by social actions, is directed at other people and designed to provoke a response.

Antisocial behavior refers to behavior that may cause harm to the society.

Types of social behaviour :

Some selected social behaviours manifested by individuals are discussed below:

- **Aggression**: It refers to the behaviour between members of the same species with an intention to hurt, ridicule or humiliate the other person. Ferguson and Beaver (2009) defined aggressive behaviour as behaviour which is intended to increase the social dominance of the organism relative to the dominance position of other organisms.
- **Altruism:** Altruism refers to a feeling of concern, sympathy and benevolence for others. It is a traditional virtue in some cultures or can be an inbuilt part of religious expectations that the followers feel motivated for.
- **Scapegoating**: Scapegoating is the practice of isolation of any party for derogatory or negative treatment or blame. Anyone can be a prey to scapegoating, a child, peer, cultural or ethnic group, worker or a country.
- **Shyness**: Shyness is a feeling of discomfort, nervousness, lack of confidence or awkwardness when a person is in the proximity (especially in a situation where one has to deal with) of an unfamiliar person.

An unusually high feeling of shyness is referred to as social phobia.

Factors influencing social behavior :

The way men behave is largely determined by their relation to each other and by their membership in groups. Culture also plays a central role in determining the social behaviour of individuals.

Social norms: The behaviour of individuals is largely influenced by social norms. Different societies have different social norms that are primary influences on the behaviour of an individual.

For example, a woman does not communicate freely in the presence of the father-in-law in North Indian societies;

- **Culture and social customs:** Culture and social customs are another important factors influencing an individual's social behaviour. For example, it is culturally not permitted to talk to elders with eye contact in the Indian society. In Western societies, however, talking to elders without maintaining proper eye contact is considered a sign of disrespect.
- **Values:** Individuals carry specific inherent values acquired from their parents, family, mentors and educational institutions. These inherent values significantly influence the social behaviour of individuals. For example, an individual having a value of not disobeying or arguing with anyone superior to him in hierarchy, either at work or community, is going to be governed by the values he or she owes.

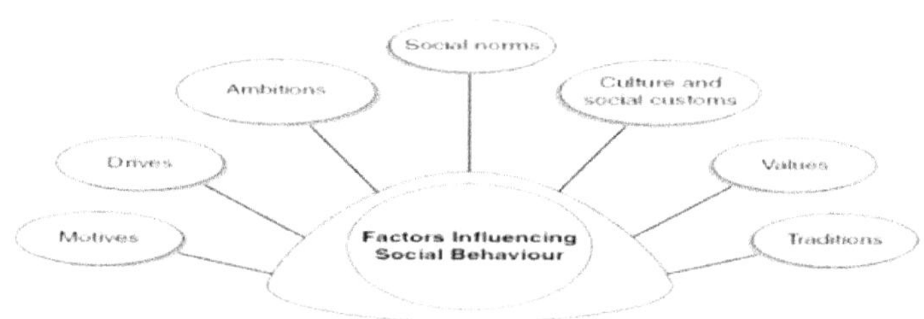

Factors influencing social behaviour.

• **Traditions:** Different societies have different traditions that are largely responsible for the overall social behaviour of individuals. For example, newly married women are expected to wear a particular type of dress and behave in a particular manner in some North Indian societies. Such traditions are certainly responsible for an individual's social behaviour.

• **Motives:** An individual's motive also significantly influences his or her social behaviour because motive governs the attitude as well as the psyche of an individual

• **Drives:** Drive may be defined as an aroused awareness, tendency or a state of heightened tension in individuals that sets off reactions and sustains the reactions for increasing the general activity level of individuals. The drive starts from within the individuals and directs them to do things that may bring about the satisfaction of that need. The strength of a drive depends upon the strength of the stimuli generated by the related need.

• **Ambitions:** An individual's ambition influences social behaviour as it gives a way to expect and respond to others. Unmotivated people exhibit sluggish social behaviour while ambitious people may display warm and proactive social behaviour.

Q 3. Write down the factors which affect the nature of behavior?

= **Factors influencing social behavior :**

The way men behave is largely determined by their relation to each other and by their membership in groups. Culture also plays a central role in determining the social behaviour of individuals.

Social norms: The behaviour of individuals is largely influenced by social norms. Different societies have different social norms that are primary influences on the behaviour of an individual.

For example, a woman does not communicate freely in the presence of the father-in-law in North Indian societies;

- **Culture and social customs:** Culture and social customs are another important factors influencing an individual's social behaviour. For example, it is culturally not permitted to talk to elders with eye contact in the Indian society. In Western societies, however, talking to elders without maintaining proper eye contact is considered a sign of disrespect.
- **Values:** Individuals carry specific inherent values acquired from their parents, family, mentors and educational institutions. These inherent values significantly influence the social behaviour of individuals. For example, an individual having a value of not disobeying or arguing with anyone superior to him in hierarchy, either at work or community, is going to be governed by the values he or she owes.

Factors influencing social behaviour.

- **Traditions:** Different societies have different traditions that are largely responsible for the overall social behaviour of individuals. For example, newly married women are expected to wear a particular type of dress and behave in a particular manner in some North Indian societies. Such traditions are certainly responsible for an individual's social behaviour.

- **Motives:** An individual's motive also significantly influences his or her social behaviour because motive governs the attitude as well as the psyche of an individual
- **Drives:** Drive may be defined as an aroused awareness, tendency or a state of heightened tension in individuals that sets off reactions and sustains the reactions for increasing the general activity level of individuals. The drive starts from within the individuals and directs them to do things that may bring about the satisfaction of that need. The strength of a drive depends upon the strength of the stimuli generated by the related need.
- **Ambitions:** An individual's ambition influences social behaviour as it gives a way to expect and respond to others. Unmotivated people exhibit sluggish social behaviour while ambitious people may display warm and proactive social behaviour.

Q 4. Define Human relations. Importance of Human relations in nursing

= Human relations are fundamental in a civil society and in each profession (including psychology, social work and health care). Nurses are one of the largest groups in health care workforce and are constantly interacting with patients, their relatives, colleagues as well as other members of the multidisciplinary health care team inside and outside the health care organization.

Human relation refers to the science of applying principles of social psychology in improving the working of an organization to make it more productive and in making the worker happier to improve efficiency and satisfaction.

Human relations are the relations between human beings that are affected by many other factors and helps in the accomplishment of goals of an organization.

Human relations in nursing

Human relations in nursing refer to the relationship of nurses with colleagues and other department personnel and of nurses with patient.

Professional relationships are created through the nurse's application of knowledge and understanding of the human behaviour as well as his or her communication and commitment to ethical behaviour.

• Nurse–patient helping relationships: Helping relationships are the foundations of clinical nursing practice. The nurse assumes the role of a professional helper in such relationships and comes to know the patient as an individual with unique health needs, human responses and patterns of living. The nurse's therapeutic use of communication helps patients overcome their problems by achieving optimum health.

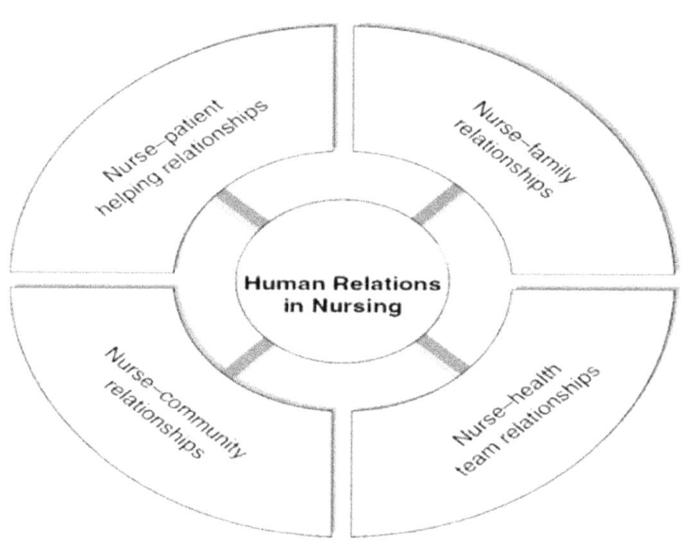

of human relations in nursing.

• Nurse–family relationships: Many nursing situations, especially those in community and home care settings, require the nurse to form helping relationships with the patient's entire family.

- Nurse–family relationships: Many nursing situations, especially those in community and home care settings, require the nurse to form helping relationships with the patient's entire family.
- Nurse–community relationships: Many nurses form relationships with community groups by participating in local organizations, volunteering for community service or by becoming politically active nurses in a community-based practice. They must be able to establish relationships with their community to be effective change agents.

Q 4. Discuss the human relations in context of Nursing.

= Human relations are fundamental in a civil society and in each profession (including psychology, social work and health care). Nurses are one of the largest groups in health care workforce and are constantly interacting with patients, their relatives, colleagues as well as other members of the multidisciplinary health care team inside and outside the health care organization.

Human relation refers to the science of applying principles of social psychology in improving the working of an organization to make it more productive and in making the worker happier to improve efficiency and satisfaction.

Human relations are the relations between human beings that are affected by many other factors and helps in the accomplishment of goals of an organization.

Human relations in nursing

Human relations in nursing refer to the relationship of nurses with colleagues and other department personnel and of nurses with patient.

Professional relationships are created through the nurse's application of knowledge and understanding of the human behaviour as well as his or her communication and commitment to ethical behaviour.

• Nurse–patient helping relationships: Helping relationships are the foundations of clinical nursing practice. The nurse assumes the role of a professional helper in such relationships and comes to know the patient as an individual with unique health needs, human responses and patterns of living. The nurse's therapeutic use of communication helps patients overcome their problems by achieving optimum health.

• Nurse–family relationships: Many nursing situations, especially those in community and home care settings, require the nurse to form helping relationships with the patient's entire family.

• Nurse–family relationships: Many nursing situations, especially those in community and home care settings, require the nurse to form helping relationships with the patient's entire family.

• Nurse–community relationships: Many nurses form relationships with community groups by participating in local organizations, volunteering for community service or by becoming politically active nurses in a community-based practice. They must be able to establish relationships with their community to be effective change agents.

Q 5. Explain the strategies to develop effective human relations in the context of nursing.

= Strategies to promote cardinal human relations

Creating positive human relations in an organization is not an easy task. However, they can be created and promoted with the help of the following suggested strategies:

• Common organizational goals: There must be promotion of a common goal perception in personnel working in an organization, so that human relations can be strengthened further.

• Group cohesiveness: Group cohesiveness in the personnel may be helpful in generating the 'we' feeling and promoting positive human relations in a group of workers.

• Effective communication practices: Effective communication practices in an organization are the key for establishing positive human relations. Therefore, to create a positive human relation environment in an organization, it is essential to practice efficient communication practices.

• Defined organizational structure: A well-defined organizational structure can affect human relations in an organization. There should be a sound organizational structure mentioning duties, expectations and job responsibilities clearly for everyone.

• Strengthening a sense of oneness: Inculcating and strengthening a sense of oneness in employees in an organization helps establish positive human relations, which ultimately benefit the organization achieve organizational goals.

• Training and skill building in human relations: In the modern health care industry, it is believed that employees can be trained and their skills built pertaining to human relations to achieve a constructive organizational environment.

• Policies to promote coordination and cooperation among employees: Each institution must have policies and procedures to promote coordination and cooperation within their employees so that a positive human relation milieu can be created. To have effective human relations, the policy framer should keep in mind that human beings have emotions, drives, thoughts and feelings (the instinct of security and possession, etc.).

Q 6. Define motivation.

= Motivation is derived from the Latin word movere which means 'to move' or 'to energize' or 'to activate'. It is a process that produces energy or drive in the individual to proceed with an activity.

Definitions of motivation

Motivation is the process of arousing the action, sustaining the activity in process and regulating the pattern of activity.

—Young

Motivation refers to the states within a person or animal that drives behavior toward some goals.

—Morgan and King

Concept of motivation

Motivation refers to sparking the personnel with zeal to perform a task for the achievement of established organizational goals. Motivation is not restricted to the sole achievement of a goal.

In fact, it inculcates the spirit of working efficiently and wholeheartedly with grit to achieve desired objectives. To accomplish this level of working, the manager needs to give positive reinforcement to various personnel.

The manager has to be consistent in figuring out areas of deficit and lack of infrastructure and provide incentives and perks with the desired appreciation to keep the personnel's morale high for a fruitful result.

Apart from providing incentives, making the personnel more decisive and giving exposure to best circumstances also prove to be lubricants for having a fruitful outcome.

In addition, personnel's individuality cannot be neglected and they should be provided with freedom of expression and a chance to work the way they want.

Q 6. Classify motives.

= According to Maslow, each of us is motivated by needs. Our most basic needs are inborn, having evolved over tens of thousands of years. The model helps explain how these needs motivate all of us. It states that we must satisfy each need, starting with the first need that deals with the most obvious need, for survival itself.

Only when the lower-order needs of physical and emotional well-being are satisfied are we concerned with the higher-order needs of influence and personal development.

Conversely, if the things satisfying our lower-order needs are swept away, we are no longer concerned about the maintenance of our higher-order needs.

The original version of this model consists of five needs discussed below :

• Basic physiological needs: The needs related to the existence and maintenance of human life are our basic physiological needs. These include things such as food, clothing, shelter, air, water and other necessities of life.

• Safety and security needs: After being content with basic needs, there is a drift towards financial and personal security and insurance.

Maslow's Hierarchy of Needs model.

• Social needs: After the satisfaction of our security needs, our needs move towards being social. These needs include interaction, adoration, respect, belongingness, etc.

• Esteem and status needs: These needs include self-respect, reputation, confidence, self-reliance, achievement, finesse, etc., and take priority after our social needs are met.

• Self-realization: Self-realization refers to the need for realizing personal potential, self-fulfilment, seeking personal growth and peak experiences. Achievement of these needs give a high degree of contentment, and complacency if they prove to be an uphill task to perform.

Q 7. Discuss the group dynamics and basic stages of group development.

= GROUP DYNAMICS

"Never doubt that a small group of thoughtful citizens can change the world. Indeed, it is the only thing that ever has" - Margaret Mead Kurt Lewin, Social Psychologist is the founder of Group Dynamics.

Group dynamics is a critical factor in group performance. Understanding how the group works and if and how it is developing will help the team leader to lead the team better. In organizational development context,

The need for managing or improving the group dynamic will lead to an intervention best consulting project where tools such as team building or socio mapping are used

Definitions

The social process by which people interact and behave in a group environment .

The study of group and also general term for foreign group process.

Group Development 'The appointment of individuals to a group based on their compatibility, diversity or expertise does not assure effectiveness in achieving group goals.

A group is initially a collection of personalities with different characteristics, needs and influences. To be effective, these individuals must spend time acclimatizing themselves to their environment, the task, and to each other.

Stages Organizational experts and practitioners have observed that new groups go through a number of stages before they achieve maximum performance. Each stage presents the members with different challenges that must overcome before they can move on to the next stage.

These stages are

1. Forming: At this first stage of development, members are pre-occupied with familiarizing themselves with the task and to other members of the group. This is sometimes referred to as the dependent stage, as members tend to depend on outside expertise for guidance, job definition, and task analysis.

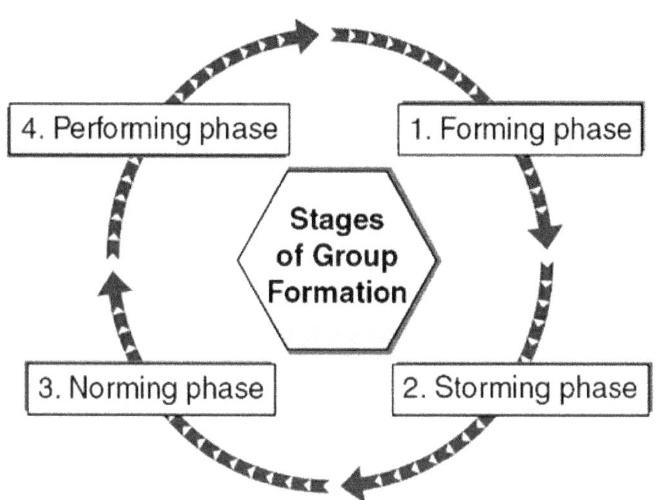

Stages of group development.

2. Storming: At this stage, the group encounters conflict as members confront and criticize each other and the approach the

group is taking to their task. Issues that arise include identification of roles and responsibilities operational rules and procedures and the individual need for recognition of his / her or her skills and abilities This stage is also referred to as the "Counter dependent stage where members tend to" flex their muscles in search of identity. In some cases, the group may have problems getting through this stage. This may occur if the group encounters difficulty clarifying their task, agreeing on their mission or mandate or deciding how they will proceed. Lack of skills, ability or aptitude can also contribute to their inability to get beyond this stage.

3. Norming: At this point, members start to resolve issues that are creating the conflict and begin to develop their social agreements. The members begin to recognize their interdependence, develop cohesion and agree on the group norms that will help them to function effectively in the future.

4. Performing: When the group has sorted out its social structure and understands its goals and individual roles, it will move towards accomplishing its task. Mutual assistance and creativity become prominent themes at this stage. The group, sensing its growth and maturity, becomes independent, relying on its own resources

5. Adjourning: During this phase, the group will resort to some form of closure that includes rites and rituals suitable to the event. These may inculed social practice ceremonies that exhibit emotiona support or celebration of the success .

Q 9. Importance of Team work in nursing.

= Teamwork divides the task and multiplies the success. It is also said that coming together is a beginning, keeping together is progress and working together is success.

Teamwork is an action performed by a team towards a common goal. A team consists of more than one person, and each person typically has different responsibilities.

The nurse leader can motivate practising nurses by encouraging teamwork. A team can be built from work groups to discuss and resolve work-related issues. Teams should have an identifiable output, inclusive membership, leaders with carefully circumscribed authority, agreement on purpose, rules of procedure and measurable goals, resources and feedback.

Teams are successful because they pool interpersonal skills, knowledge and expertise to accomplish goals effectively and efficiently.

Teamwork can be defined as a dynamic process involving two or more health care professionals with complementary backgrounds and skills, sharing common health goals and exercising concerted physical and mental effort in assessing, planning or evaluating patient care in health care.

Importance of Team work in nursing.

Teamwork gives a better end result with high-quality performance from each team member.

• Teamwork involves every person and his expertise and responsibilities.

• The execution of new ideas can be more effective and efficient through teamwork

. • Teamwork increases ownership with wider communication.

• Teamwork leads to information sharing and increases learning in the team and the organization.

• Teamwork provides more security and develops personal relationships in the context of business operations.

• A particular problem can be easily solved in a team with more ideas at the same time.

• Teamwork helps provide a variety of solutions and the best solution from those possibilities can be selected.

• Teamwork increases the willingness of every member to take more risk. • People can share common goals and interests with others in the team.

• It is easier to examine problems and identify various solutions in a team.

- A team can handle more difficult and complex problems in the workplace.
- A team increases the accuracy of problem solving.

CHAPTER FOUR

GUIDENCE & COUNSELING

SHORT ANSWER QUESTIONS

Q 1. Crisis management process.

= The word crisis comes from two Chinese words; Danger and Opportunity. Danger Opportunity Crisis .

Crisis is any event that is expected to lead to, an unstable and dangerous situation affecting an individual, group, or whole organization

Crisis Management • Crisis Management: is the process by which an organization deals with a major event that threatens to harm the organization, its stakeholders, or the general public.

Crisis Management Cycle Identification Preparation Prevention Response Recovery Learning

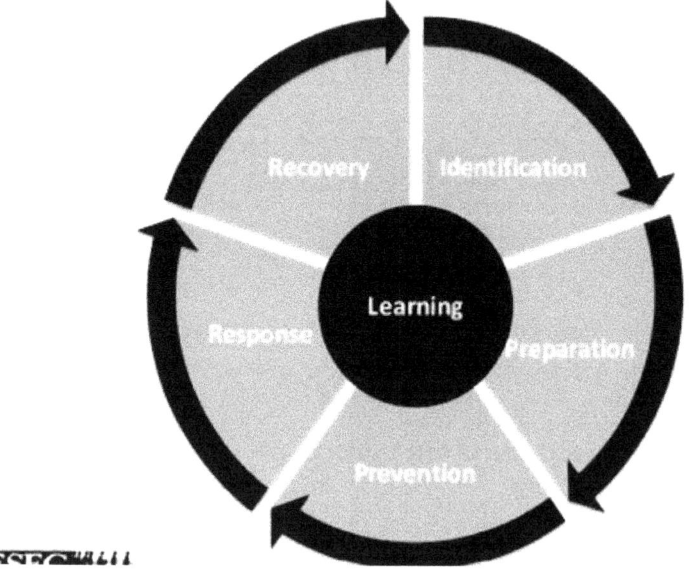

Identification

• First Stage of crisis management is **IDENTIFYING** the crisis' nature.

• Crisis can be clustered into:

– Natural crisis: occur due to natural disasters.

– Organizational Misdeed crisis: occur when management take actions that harm stakeholders without suitable precautions.

– Deception crisis: occur due to lack of transparency from the management about certain information.

– Workplace violence crisis: occur when member commit violence to other members.

– Skewed values crisis: occur when short- term gain is favored and values are neglected.

– Rumors crisis: occur when false information about an organization and its product hurt the organization's reputation.

• Second Stage is **PREPARING** for the crisis.

• Crisis preparation is done by:

– Vulnerability Assessment: determine current and potential areas of operational and communications weakness.

– Crisis Planning: are two types

• Operational : What we do, who does it, and when it is done.

• Communications: what do we say, who says it, how do we get the messages out. Preparation

• Third stage is **PREVENTING** the crisis from happening.

• Crisis Prevention is occurred by:

– Anticipate and Have a plan.

– Respond immediately.

– Do not over talk.

– Always tell the truth.

– Accept responsibility. Prevention

• Fourth stage is **RESPONDING** to the crisis.

• Effective crisis response includes:

– Set of planning scenarios.

– Set of response modules.

– Preset activation protocols.

– Clear communication channels. Response

• Fifth stage is **RECOVERING** from the crisis.

Organizations must be able to carry on with their business in the middle of the crisis.

while simultaneously planning for how they will recover from the damage the crisis caused.

Crisis handlers must engage in the recovery plan while perusing the goal. Recovery

Q 3. Differences between counseling and guidance.

= **Guidance**

"A process through which an individual is able to solve their problems and pursue a path suited to their abilities and aspirations" **-JM Brewer.**

"An educational service designed to help students make more effective use of the schools and training program" **-Educational Point of View**

Counseling :

DEFINITIONS Counseling

A helping process where one person, explicitly and purposefully gives his / her time, attention and skills assist a client to explore the situation, identify and act upon solutions within the limitations of their gires environment

"A method that helps the client to use a problem - solving process to recognize and manage stress interpersonal relationships among client, family and health care team

DIFFERENCE BETWEEN GUIDANCE AND COUNSELLING

GUIDANCE	COUNSELLING
Guidance is broader & comprehensive	Counselling is in-depth & narrow
Guidance is more external, helps a person understand alternative solutions available to him & makes him understand his personality & choose the right solution.	Counselling helps people understand themselves & is an inward analysis. Alternative solutions are proposed to help understand the problem at hand.
Guidance is mainly preventive & developmental	Counselling is remedial as well as preventive & developmental

DIFFERENCE BETWEEN GUIDANCE AND COUNSELLING

GUIDANCE	COUNSELLING
Intellectual attitudes are the raw material of guidance	Emotional rather than pure intellectual attitude are raw material of the counselling process.
Decision making is operable at an intellectual level in guidance	Counselling operates at an emotional level
Guidance is generally education & career related & may also be for personal problems	Counselling is mostly offered for personal & social issues.

Basis for Comparison	Guidance	COUNSELLING
Meaning	Guidance refers to an advice or a relevant piece of information provided by a superior, to resolve a problem or overcome from difficulty.	Counselling refers to a professional advice given by a counselor to an individual to help him in overcoming from personal or psychological problems.
Nature	Preventive	Remedial and Curative
Approach	Comprehensive and Extroverted	In-depth and Introverted
What it does?	It assists the person in choosing the best alternative.	It tends to change the perspective, to help him get the solution by himself or herself.
Deals with	Education and career related issues.	Personal and socio-psychological issues.
Provided by	Any person superior or expert	A person who possesses high level of skill and professional training.
Privacy	Open and less private.	Confidential
Mode	One to one or one to many	One to one
Decision making	By guide.	By the client.

Q 4. Classify the various types of crisis.

= Crisis is a state of disequilibrium resulting from the interaction of an event with the individual's or family's coping mechanisms, which are inadequate to meet the demands of the situation, combined with the individual's or family's perception of the meaning of the event. - Taylor, 1982

DEFINITION : Crisis as A dramatic emotional or circumstantial upheaval in a personal life and a stage in a sequence of events at which the trend of all future events ,especially for better or determined, a turning point.

TYPES OF CRISIS :

There are three types of crisis

(1)Maturational or developmental crisis

(2)Situational crisis

(3)Adventitious crisis

(1) DEVELOPMENTAL CRISIS

Developmental crisis (also referred to as maturational or internal crisis) may occur at any transitional period in normal growth and development.

The transitional periods where individuals move into successive stage often generate disequilibrium.

Individuals are required to make cognitive and behavioural changes that accompany development, precipitate factors are normal stress of development (eg. adolescence Retirement ,marriage and parenthood)

(2)SITUATIONAL CRISIS:

A situational crisis (sometimes called accidental or external crisis) is a response to a sudden and unavoidable traumatic event that largely affects a person's identity and roles.

Examplles of events that can participate situational crisis are sudden traumatic event.(eg.unexpected job loss ,serious car accidents,ioss of spouse,academic failure,birth of a child with a disability or diagnosis with a chronic or terminal illness) affects how people perceive themselves.

(3)Adventitious crisis (social crisis) :

Social crisis is accidential, uncommon and unanticipated and result in multiple losses and radical environmental changes. ?An adventitious crisis occurs outside the person precipitate by an unexpected event. (eg.Natural disaster,fires,floods,war etc.)

These crises affect many people who experience both acute and post traumatic stress reaction.

This type of crisis is unlike maturational and situational crisis because it doesn't occur in the lives of all people.

Q 5. Define guidance and counseling

= **DEFINITIONS Guidance**

"A process of dynamic interpersonal relationships designed to influence the attitudes and subsequent behavior of a person" **-Good.**

"Assistance made available by qualified and adequately trained personnel to an individual of any age to help an individual to manage his own life activities, to develop his own points of view, make his own decisions and carry his own steps to solve the problems" - **Crow and Crow.**

"A process through which an individual is able to solve their problems and pursue a path suited to their abilities and aspirations" **-JM Brewer.**

"An educational service designed to help students make more effective use of the schools and training program" **-Educational Point of View**

DEFINITIONS Counseling

A helping process where one person, explicitly and purposefully gives his / her time, attention and skills assist a client to explore the situation, identify and act upon solutions within the limitations of their gires environment

"A method that helps the client to use a problem - solving process to recognize and manage stress interpersonal relationships among client, family and health care team

"" Consultation, mutual interchange of opinions deliberating together"

Q 6. Explain the elements of counseling process

= "A method that helps the client to use a problem - solving process to recognize and manage stress interpersonal relationships among client, family and health care team

"" Consultation, mutual interchange of opinions deliberating together"

Elements in Counseling Process Counseling involves two individuals ;

it is a communication between the counselor and counselee (i .e.Tone of voice , facial expressions , gestures and postures of both play an important role) .

Counselor - A professionally trained person who can assist or help the counselee .

Counselee - A person who seeks help or needs assistance . Mutual respect , rapport and satisfactory relationship should be established .

Counselor should be friendly and cooperative with counselee . Counselee should have trust and confidence over the counselor . Counselor should have thorough experience and sound knowledge with counseling process .

It concerns itself with attitudes and actions , Information ; intellectual attitudes , understanding of e...

Ask the client to get family and friend's support . Get or refer to consultation , when it is beyond the skills of counselor . Maintain confidentiality , counseling interview must be structured .

Q 7.Write down the basic principles of counseling.

= "A method that helps the client to use a problem - solving process to recognize and manage stress interpersonal relationships among client, family and health care team

"" Consultation, mutual interchange of opinions deliberating together"

Basic Principles of Counseling Process

According to Mc Daniel and Shaftal, the counseling process is based on some basic principles:

(a) Principle of Acceptance:

According to this principle, each client must the accepted as an individual and dealt with as such. The counselor should give, due regard to the rights of the client.

(b) Principle of Permissiveness:

Counseling is such a relationship which develops optimism and the environment shapes according to the person. All the thoughts accept the relative relationship of counseling.

(c) Principle of Respect for the Individual:

All the schools of thoughts of counseling advocate for the respect of the individual i.e., respecting an individual's feelings must be an integral part of counseling process.

(d) Principle of Thinking with the Individual:

Counseling emphasizes thinking with the individual. It is essential to differentiate think for whom? And 'why to think'? It is the role of the counselor the think about all the forces around the client to join client's thought process and to work collectively with the client regarding his problem.

(e) Principle of Learning:

All the assumptions of counseling accept the presence of learning- elements in the counseling process.

(f) Principle of Consistency with Ideals of Democracy:

All the principles are associated with ideals of democracy. The ideals of democracy desire to accept a person and want to respect the rights of others.

The process of counseling is based upon the ideals of a person's respect. It is a process with accepts individual differences.

Q 8.Write the areas of counseling in nursing education.

= "A method that helps the client to use a problem - solving process to recognize and manage stress interpersonal relationships among client, family and health care team

"" Consultation, mutual interchange of opinions deliberating together"

Need of Guidance and Counselling in Nursing Education...

1. To help students adjusting with the new environment of the nursing institute.
2. To help in developing qualities required for a successful for a nursing practice.
3. To help students in getting adjusted with the clinical environment.
4. To help students keeping in touch with the latest trends in nursing
5. To help students in developing positive learning habits, especially skill learning

6. To help in the development of appropriate coping straggles in order to deal with stress in a productive manner
7. To help nursing students in establishing proper identity.
8. To help them to develop a positive attitude towards life.
9. To help to overcome periods of turmoil & confusion.
10. To help students in developing their leadership qualities.
11. To motivate them for taking membership in professional organizations after competing their studies.
12. Helps them to make advantages of technological advancement in a patient care.
13. Helps them to readiness for changes & face challenges
14. To carryout responsibilities as a health team member
15. Helps them to proper selection of career
16. Motivate them for higher studies.

Q 9. Explain the techniques of counseling.

= "A method that helps the client to use a problem - solving process to recognize and manage stress interpersonal relationships among client, family and health care team

"" Consultation, mutual interchange of opinions deliberating together"

Phase 1 Establish relationship phase –

1 : Establishing relationship Is the core phase in the process of counseling . It affects the progress of the process and acts as a curative not possible to have a generalized relationship . It includes factors like : respect , trust and comfort etc agetal mn itsclf . It should be recognised that each counsclee - counselor relationship is unique and hence it is

Begin the phase with adequate social skills

• Introduce yourself

Listen attentively and remember the client's name

Ensure physical comfort

Always address the individual by his / her preferred name

Do not interrupt the individual while he / she is talking

Observe non - verbal communications , becomes comfortable with you and accepts you into her / his inner world .

The relationship is not established in just a single session but may require several sessions before he / she became a comfortable with you and accept you into her inner world.

Phase - 2 . Assessment

it is a phase in which individuals are encouraged to talk about their problems ; counselor asks questions Observations problem . collects information , seeks his / her views , observes and possibly helps the individual to clearly state his / her This is the data collecting phase and involves several specific skills such as :

- Enquiry .
- Making associations among facts
- Recording
- Making educated guesses
- Recording the information systematically and promptly .

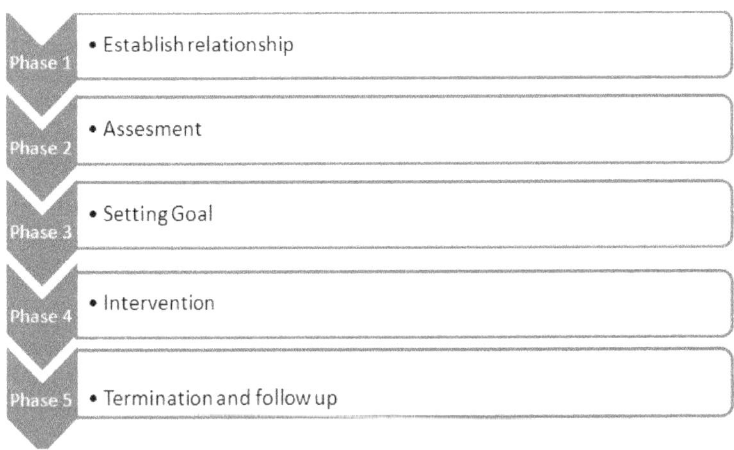

Phase 3 : Setting Goals

The purpose of this phase is to provide direction to the individual and counselor . It involves making a commitment to a set of conditions , a course of action or an outcome . Setting goals helps to know how well counseling is working and when counseling may be concluded . Setting gouts

Two types -- Immediate and ultimate .

- The process of setting goals is cooperately done by the counselor and the individual . It requires :
- The skills of drawing inference
- Differentiation
- Teaching individuals to think realistically

It should be emphasized that goals are not fixed for all time to come and can be changed whenever new normation is received or new insight is developed .

Pase - 4 : Intervention

as a phase which is more influened by the view points a counselor holds about the counseling process . After setting goals the question that follows is 'how shall we accomplish these goals?' the intervention used will depend upon the approach used by the counselor , the problem and the individual . Hence the choice of the intervention is a process of adaption and the counselor should change the intervention when the selected intervention is not working . This is similar to medical treatment . When one treatment does not work the practitioner tries the alternative treatment . The counseling skills needed are skill in handling the interventions knowledge of its effects and ability to read client's reactions . Individuals can be asked in the beginning about what interventions they have earlier so that other interventions can be used .

Phase - 5 : Termination and Follow - up

All counseling has its ultimate criterion a successful termination . It must be done without destroying the accomplishments gained and should be done with sensitivity , intention and by fading . It is not unusual for the individual to have a feeling of a sense loss , hence termination should be planned over few sessions . Follow -up appointments can also be fixed for sometime .

Q 10. Explain the principles of counseling .

= "A method that helps the client to use a problem - solving process to recognize and manage stress interpersonal relationships among client, family and health care team

"" Consultation, mutual interchange of opinions deliberating together"

Principles to be followed in Counseling technique

1. **Acceptance :** The client should not be hindered in any manner ; he / she should be fully encouraged to express his / her feelings freely .

2. **Restatement :** The Counselor should enable the counselee to realize that he / she is being fully understood and accepted

3. **Clarification :** The counselor tries to give correct information , clarifies the doubts of counselee .

4. **Reassurance :** Confidence in counseling being given to him / her , reassures the client about the effectiveness of counseling

5. **Interpretation :** To develop insight by the counselee , he / she understands the unconscious motives that he she resolves his / her inner conflicts .

6. **Advice :** Advice should be given only in those causes where it is sought for .

7. **Rejection :** It reverses the direction of thoughts of counselee .

8. **Lead :** The client is asked a question in a manner that is helpful to him / her in determining the answer .

Q 11 Discuss the Qualities / attributes of counselor.

= A counsellor is a person whose job is to give advice to people who need it, especially advice on their personal problems.

1.Professional Qualities:

He knows the demands and responsibilities of the counselling profession.

He knows the aims and objectives of counselling.

He is aware of the steps and techniques involved in the counselling process.

He has the best interest of the counselee in mind and receives the trust of the counselee.

He is confident and well versed in the methods and approaches of counselling

2.Personal Qualities:

The counsellor respects the client's individuality and dignity

He knows the psychology of each client, how they think and behave.

He is kind and sympathetic to clients' problems and anxieties

He is gentle, especially when sorting out corrective measures.

He is dignified and neat in his manners, speech and appearance.

He is in control of his emotions especially of anger, impatience and frustrations.

He is able to use humour and laughter in his counselling, laugh with clients, not laugh at them or them at him.

3.Communication Skills:

Effective counsellors should have excellent communication skills. Counsellors' need to have a natural ability to listen and be able clearly explain their ideas and thoughts to others. 4. Acceptance: The ability to relate to clients with an open, nonjudgmental attitude -- accepting the client for who she is and in her current situation. Counsellors need to be able to convey acceptance to their clients with warmth and understanding.

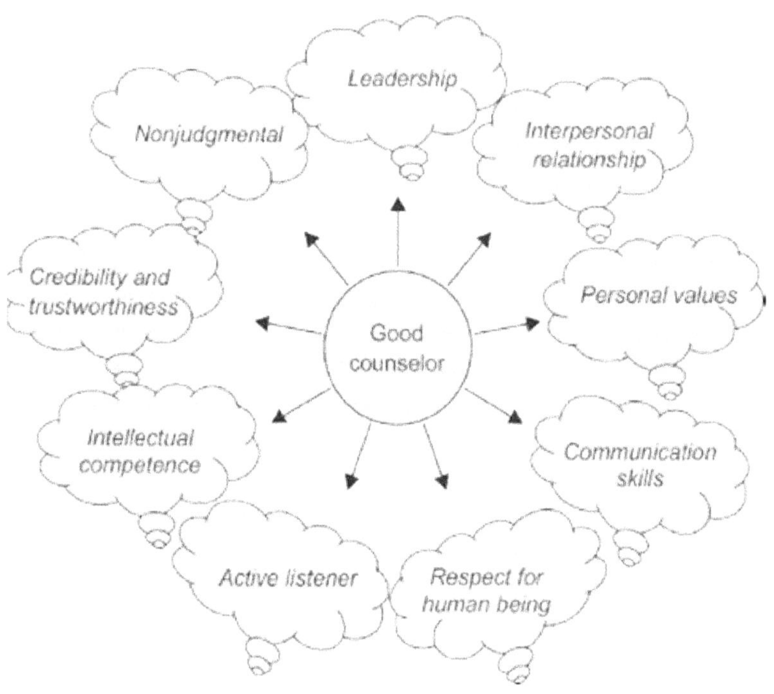

4.Empathy:

Counsellors must be able to display empathy -- the ability to feel what another person is feeling. Empathy means that you are truly able to imagine what it's like to stand in someone else's shoes. Compassion and empathy help your clients feel understood and heard. 6. Problem-Solving Skills: It's not up to a counsellor to solve her clients' problems, no matter how much she might want to help. But counsellors must have excellent problem-solving skills to be able to help their clients identify and make changes to negative thought patterns and other harmful behaviours.

5 .Rapport-Building Skills:

Counsellors must possess a strong set of interpersonal skills to help establish rapport with clients and develop strong relationships.

Counsellors need to be able to place all of their focus on what their clients are saying and avoid being distracted by their own personal problems or concerns when they are in a session.

6 .Flexibility:

Flexibility in counselling is defined as the ability to adapt and change the way you respond to meet your clients' needs. You don't stay rigid and stick to a predetermined treatment path when your clients require a different approach. Being flexible is one of the most important attributes of a professional counsellor

7.Self-Awareness:

Self-awareness is the ability to look within and identify your own unmet psychological needs and desires, such as a need for intimacy or the desire to be professionally competent. This ability prevents your issues from affecting or conflicting with those of your clients. Self-awareness has a major impact on a counsellor's effectiveness.

8.Multicultural Competency:

Counsellors help people from all walks of life. Multicultural competency means that you try to relate to and understand your clients regardless of their race, ethnicity, religious or political beliefs or socioeconomic background.

9.Conclusion :

In addition to all the qualities mentioned above, the counsellor must have qualities of a good personality, good character and wholesome philosophy, health, emotional stability, approachability, intelligence, broad knowledge and interest in guidance and personal working conditions and understanding of social economic conditions. In short, a counsellor should have qualities of head and heart. It is wiser to say, 'Counselling is more of a heart-matter than a head-matter.'

Q 12. Explain the different types of counseling services.

= Counseling is a specialized service of guidance, and it is an enabling process designed to help through learning to take responsibility and to make decisions for himself / herself. It is a helping relationship which includes

Someone seeking help

Someone willing to give help

TYPES OF COUNSELLING

1. Directive Counselling :

An approach to counseling and psychotherapy in which the therapeutic process is directed along lines considered relevant by the counselor or therapist. Directive counseling is based on the assumption that the professional training and experience of the counselor or therapist equip him or her to manage the therapeutic process and to guide the client's behavior. Also called **directive therapy**

1. **Non Directive Counselling / client centred Counselling :Non-Directive Counselling**: In this type of **counselling** the counselee or client or pupil, not the **counsellor** is the pivot of the **counselling** process. ... Since the counsellee is given full freedom to talk about his problems and work out a solution, this technique is also called the "permissive" **counselling**.

3. Short Term Counselling :Short-term counselling – also known as brief **therapy** or time-limited **therapy** – typically refers to solution-based **therapy** with a distinct goal in mind (for example, looking at patterns of negative thinking). Often having a tighter focus than **long-term therapy**, **short-term** sessions typically span six to twelve sessions.

4. Long Term Counselling :Long-term psychotherapy is typically referred to as **psychotherapy** that exceeds the normal parameters of time allotted for the treatment of most psychological disorders.

5. Psychological counselling : **Counseling psychologists** help people with physical, emotional and mental health issues improve their sense of well-being, alleviate feelings of distress

6. **Clinical Counselling :Clinical counseling** is a branch of **clinical** psychology that helps people as they navigate emotional or **mental health** difficulties. **Clinical counseling** can also be considered part of professional **counseling** and social work fields.

7. **Student Counselling :** Student Counselling Cell aims to help students become self-aware and reach their highest potential while dealing with anxiety and stress. The counselling cell provides a happy and comfortable environment for students to discuss their problems regarding their academic and social life.

8. Placement Counselling

9) **Marriage Counselling :Marriage counselling**, sometimes known as **couples therapy**, helps **couples** (whether **married** or not) to understand and resolve their conflicts and improve their relationship **with each other.**

10) Vocational counselling

11) Psycho therapeutic counselling

12) Individual Counselling

13) Group counselling

14) Behavioral counselling

15) Dietary counselling

16) Motivational counselling

27. 17)Interpersonal counselling

18)Problem solving counselling

19)Educational counselling : the counseling specialty **concerned with providing advice and assistance to students** in the development of their educational plans, choice of appropriate courses, and choice of college or technical school. Also called educational guidance;

20)Personal counselling

21)Moral, religious and social counseling

Q 13. Mention the type of a guidance required for nursing students.

= "A method that helps the client to use a problem - solving process to recognize and manage stress interpersonal relationships among client, family and health care team

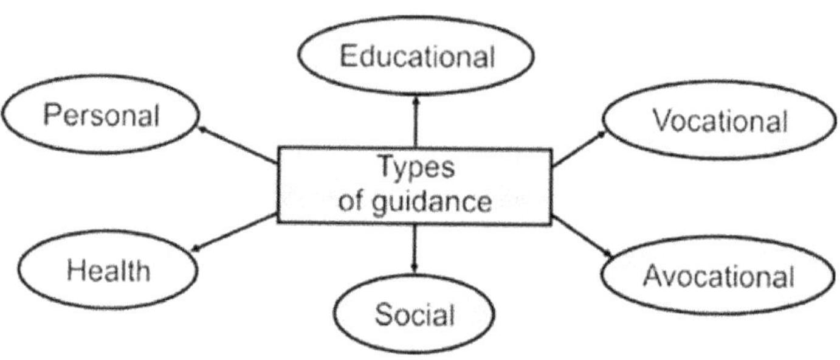

Health Guidance : This guidance is the assistance offered to the individual to solve their emotional , social , ethical and moral as well as health problem .

Q 14 Write the scope of guidance and counseling in nursing education.

= **SCOPE OF GUIDANCE AND COUNSELLING**

- Guidance & counselling for personal needs/problems
- Guidance & counselling for physical, emotional, social, moral & marital problems
- Guidance & counselling for career advancement
- Guidance & counselling for educational needs/problems
- Guidance & counselling for vocational, occupational & professional needs
- Guidance & counselling for holistic individual development
- **Guidance & counselling for situational problems**

Q 14 . Purposes of counseling services.

= Counseling Services Purposes of Counseling (Dunsmoor and Miller)

Get information about the pupil which will be of help to him in solving his problems.

Give the pupil information on matters important to his success.

Help the pupil work out a plan for solving his difficulties.

Establish a feeling of mutual understanding between pupil and teacher

Encourage special talents and develop right attitudes

Help the pupil know himself better, his interests, abilities, aptitudes, and available opportunities.

Assist the pupil in planning for his educational and vocational choices

Inspire successful endeavour toward the attainment or realization of objectives

Q 15 Enlist the steps involved in counseling process.

= "A method that helps the client to use a problem - solving process to recognize and manage stress interpersonal relationships among client, family and health care team

"" Consultation, mutual interchange of opinions deliberating together"

Phase 1 Establish relationship phase –

1 : Establishing relationship Is the core phase in the process of counseling . It affects the progress of the process and acts as a curative not possible to have a generalized relationship . It includes factors like : respect , trust and comfort etc agetal mn itself . It should be recognished that each counsclee - counselor relationship is unique and hence it is

Begin the phase with adequate social skills

• Introduce yourself

Listen attentively and remember the client's name

Ensure physical comfort

Always address the individual by his / her preferred name

Do not interrupt the individual while he / she is talking

Observe non - verbal communications , becomes comfortable with you and accepts you into her / his inner world .

The relationship is not established in just a single session but may require several sessions before he / she became a comfortable with you and accept you into her inner world.

Phase - 2 . Assessment

it is a phase in which individuals are encouraged to talk about their problems ; counselor asks questions Observations problem . collects information , seeks his / her views , observes and possibly helps the individual to clearly state his / her This is the data collecting phase and involves several specific skills such as :

- Enquiry .
- Making associations among facts
- Recording
- Making educated guesses
- Recording the information systematically and promptly .

Phase 1 • Establish relationship

Phase 2 • Assesment

Phase 3 • Setting Goal

Phase 4 • Intervention

Phase 5 • Termination and follow up

Phase 3 : Setting Goals

The purpose of this phase is to provide direction to the individual and counselor . It involves making a commitment to a set of conditions , a course of action or an outcome . Setting goals helps to know how well counseling is working and when counseling may be concluded . Setting gouts

Two types -- Immediate and ultimate .

- The process of setting goals is cooperately done by the counselor and the individual . It requires :
- The skills of drawing inference
- Differentiation
- Teaching individuals to think realistically

It should be emphasized that goals are not fixed for all time to come and can be changed whenever new normation is received or new insight is developed .

Pase - 4 : Intervention

as a phase which is more influened by the view points a counselor holds about the counseling process . After setting goals the question that follows is 'how shall we accomplish these goals?' the intervention used will depend upon the approach used by the counselor , the problem and the individual . Hence the choice of the intervention is a process of adaption and the counselor should change the intervention when the selected intervention is not working . This is similar to medical treatment . When one treatment does not work the practitioner tries the alternative treatment . The counseling skills needed are skill in handling the interventions knowledge of its effects and ability to read client's reactions . Individuals can be asked in the beginning about what interventions they have earlier so that other interventions can be used .

Phase - 5 : Termination and Follow - up

All counseling has its ultimate criterion a successful termination . It must be done without destroying the accomplishments gained and should be done with sensitivity , intention and by fading . It is not unusual for the individual to have a feeling of a sense loss , hence termination should be planned over few sessions . Follow -up appointments can also be fixed for sometime .

CHAPTER FIVE

PRINCIPLES OF EDUCATION & TEACHING LEARNING PROCESS

SHORT ANSWER QUESTIONS .

Q 1. Specific aims of education .

= Definitions of education by indian philosophers Famous Indian philosophers or educationists have given the following concepts of education with their own meanings:

Education means the training for the country and love for the nation. —Chanakya

Education is realization of self. —Shankaracharya

Education is self-realization and service of the people. —Guru Nanak Dev

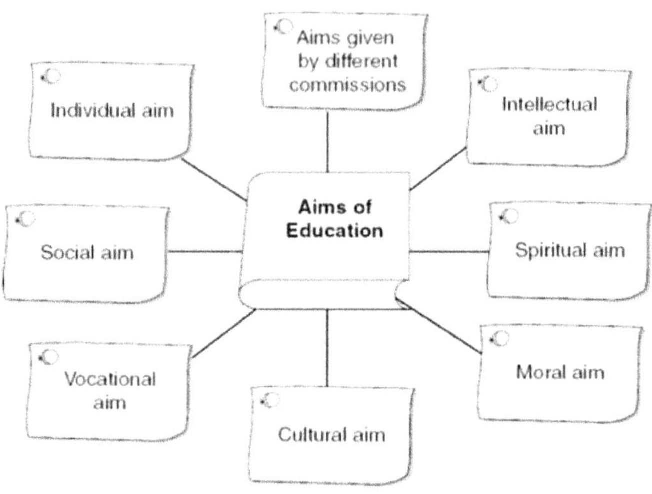

FIGURE 5.1 Aims of education.

Aims of education

Education is a purposeful and planned activity undertaken by the educator and the learner for achieving clearly defined objectives or ends in view. Without an end or objective no purposeful activity will have the real force which directs it and makes it meaningful.

Individual aim: Education should aim at the training and development of an individual. Only a well-trained individual can understand his rights and obligations towards the society.

Some important individual aims of education are as follows:

Development as an individual of a human being

- Moral and spiritual development
- Cultural development
- Harmonious development
- Promote positive physical development
- Provide a sense of complete living

- Development of a right personality
- Development of good citizenship
- Development of good leadership

Social aim :

An individual is born with certain potential and natural endowments. It is the task of education to develop these into distinct individual personality. Personality development does not take place in a vacuum. It takes place in association with others, in cooperative living and in working together for the welfare of group or society. As per historical evidences, in ancient Sparta, it was believed that each individual was born not for himself but for his country. A socially efficient individual conforms to certain standards of conduct known as moral conduct.

Vocational aim :

Education should have a utilitarian aim. This means that education should help an individual earn his livelihood himself which is an esessential function of life that cannot be ignored. This aim makes an individual economically self-sufficient, gives purpose to the educational activity and bridges the gap between pure literary education and vocation.

Cultural aim : Culture is a complete whole and includes knowledge, belief, art, morals, law, custom and other capabilities and habits acquired by man as a member of society. True education is not satisfied if members of a society take up and preserve only the existing manners and customs.

- **Moral aim:** A strong character includes physical fitness, resolution and will power. Moral virtues like honesty, loyalty, tolerance, justice, self-control and sincerity promote the social efficiency of an individual.
- **Spiritual aim:** Ancient Indian educators defined education as a means for salvation. DrRadhakrishnan said that the aim of education is neither national efficiency nor world solidarity but making individual feel that he has within himself something deeper than intellect, call it spirit, if you like. But spiritual aim does not find any place in the western education system.

Q 2.. Aims of nursing education.

= **Aims of nursing education**

Nursing education has its aims in common with the aims of education in general as well as specific. The nursing education aims are determined by the health needs of the society, needs of students, philosophy of nursing, current trends in education and nursing and advancement in science and technology. The many nursing aims are listed below:

- **Intellectual aim:** Theoretical and practical knowledge is essential for rendering intelligent and efficient nursing services. Professional nursing practice is based on scientific principles and evidence-based practice.
- **Leadership aim:** Nurses plan, organize and manage health care activities and programmes. They haveto evaluate the quality and structure of health care services. They have to coordinate and collaborate on the health care services. Thus, education aims at identifying potential nursing leaders.
- **Professional development aim:** Each individual nurse should be educated in a manner to enable her to develop the appropriate skills and attitude essential for professional practice.
- **Personality development aim**: Nursing education should aim at an all-round development of the individual in all aspects. The nurse should grow and develop as a person of self-awareness, self-direction and self-motivation.
- **Generating and utilizing research evidences:** Evidence-based practice and ongoing research is vital for the growth of the nursing profession. Therefore, nursing education must pay emphasis on the utilization and development of resource evidence.
- **Ensuring a safe, quality and cost-effective case:** It is the prime responsibility of the nursing education that it equip its professionals to provide safe, quality and cost-effective care to the common man.

Q3. Function of education.

= Functions of education Education is the process of living through a continuous reconstruction of experiences. It is the development of all those capacities in an individual which will enable him to control his environment and fulfill his possibilities.

A child is born with certain endowments which are developed in accordance with the demands of the society through education. Education enables the child to manipulate his environment. Thus, education provides important functions towards the individual as well as the society. Functions of education can solely be for an individual or to towards the society and nation at large. Some essential functions of education are discussed below .

Function of education towards an individual

Education participates in the growth and direction of an individual as described below:

Growth and development of individual:

Johann Heinrich Pestalozzi said when we leave the earth carelessly to nature, it bears weeds and thistles. The same way when we leave child's education to nature alone, he develops only confused impressions in his mind. Thus, only environmental and natural growth is not sufficient for the complete growth and development of an individual. To this must be added a systematic course of formal training. Moreover, only one-sided growth will not serve the purpose. The whole personality of the child should develop physically, intellectually, morally, socially and spiritually.

- **Direction and guidance:** Direction refers to minimizing unnecessary and confusing movements. When an immature child responds to stimulus, much of the superfluous energy is wasted. This wastage can be saved if the child's activity is properly directed towards a goal. One can be directed by his internal tendencies or by external stimulus. The teacher, therefore, in the direction programme should take into account the external factors of an environment as well as the child's inborn tendency

. • **Preparation for adult life:** Preparation of a child for the responsibilities or privileges of adult life have been considered to be the chief function of education from ancient times

. • **Conservation of traditional knowledge:** Preserving old traditions, values, ideals, customs and way of thinking is also a function of education.

Transmission of culture: Transmitting the cultural heritage to the younger generation is achieved through education.

• **Progressive development**: Reconstructing new experiences, unfolding new dimensions of knowledge and furthering civilization and culture.

• **Develop vocational efficiency**: Education enables the person to acquire the knowledge and skills to efficiently perform the tasks related to a particular vocation or professional field.

• **Achievement of self-sufficiency**: Self-sufficiency can be gained by the individual through education because after the due education person is able to earn for her own livelihood as well as become cognitively and economically independent.

• **Holistic personality development:** Education must be aimed at developing an individual's holistic personality. • Moral and character development: An ideal education must be helpful for an individual to develop good moral values and character.

• **Creating awareness of past and present and preparing for future**: Education must make an individual become knowledgeable about the past and present scenarios of social and professional pursuit as well prepare him to manage future expectations and needs.

Function of education towards the nation

National progress depends on an individual's hard work, energy, selflessness and devotion. Education plays important role to inculcate these qualities in individuals. The Kothari Commission Report rightly said that the destiny of India was being reshaped in its classroom. The important functions of education for a nation are given below:

• **Ensuring national development**: National development largely depends on the education of a country. It is directly proportional to the literacy rate as well as availability of human resources.

• **Promoting national integrity**: India is a country of diversity having a strong sense of casteism, communalism, provincialism, regionism and linguistic antagonism that could serve as barriers to national integration. Education can be helpful in breaking these barriers and can promote national integration.

• **Continuous supply of skilled workforce to the nation**: Every country requires a skilled workforce for the smooth functioning of its service sector. It is the main national function of education to ensure the continuous supply of skilled workforce to the country.

• **Developing leaders for the nation:** Leaders are the main role players in the overall development of a country. Leaders are essentially required in social,

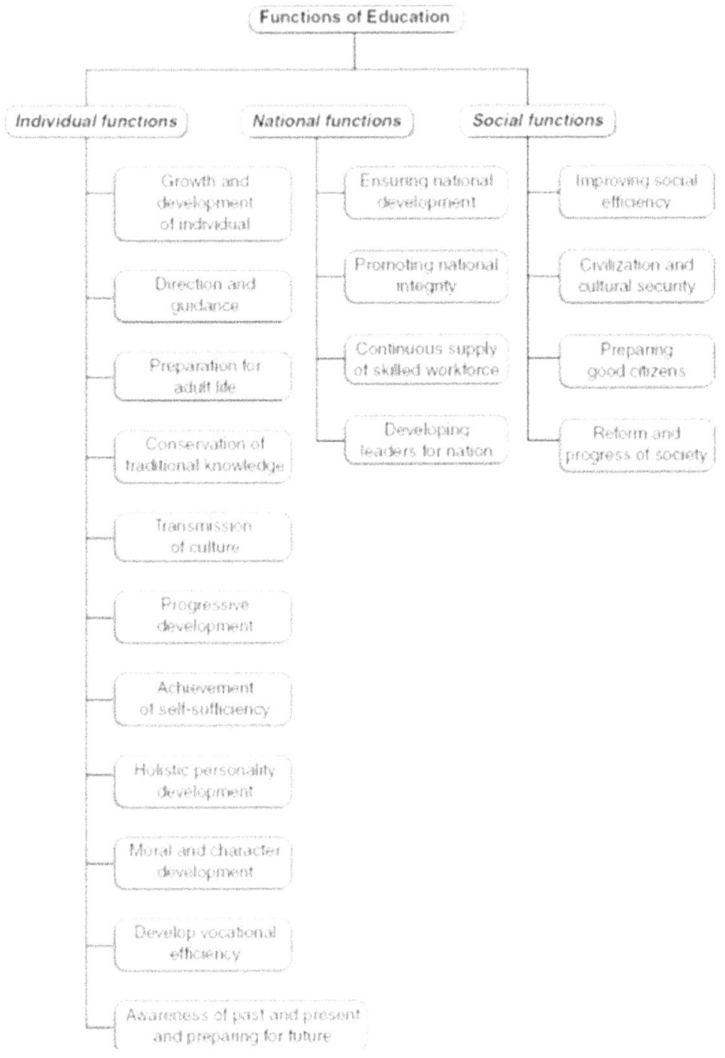

economic, political and cultural sectors and education can realize this requirement by preparing leaders to meet a country's present and future needs. III. Function of education towards the society As biological life maintains and transmits by nutrition and reproduction, the same way social life is maintained by education. Education is necessary and an inevitable result of the society's needs to guide the growth and development of its younger members to produce an improved generation. History bears evidence that as education advances, civilization also advances.

Some selected social functions of education are as follows:

- **Improving social efficiency:** Education ensures the overall holistic development of individuals, who could be good individuals in a society. It ultimately promotes social efficiency and the society flourishes in the right direction.
- **Civilization and cultural security**: Education teaches individual gain civic sense so that a positive civilization can be expected for its members. In addition, education must ensure cultural security so that important traditional culture can be preserved and utilized by the future generations.
- **Preparing good citizens:** The main function of education is to prepare good citizens in a country so that a civilized society can be expected and each individual has the privilege of enjoying full social freedom, human honour and rights.

Q 4 . Factors affecting education.

= **Factors affecting aims of education**

Educational aims are affected by certain factors such as philosophy of life, elements of human nature, religious reasons, political ideology, socioeconomic reasons, cultural reasons and the intention of exploringnew knowledge, which are described as follows :

- **Philosophy of life:** Both educational aims and philosophy of life are very closely related just like two facets of the same coin. Education is the best means of propagation of the philosophy of life and philosophy gives the basis for aims of education
- **Elements of human nature:** Human nature is always considered for determining educational aims. Idealism infolding divinity in man is considered as the main aim of education.

• **Religious factors:** Religion is an inseparable determinant of educational aims. In India, Buddhism focuses on adoption of ahimsa and truth in the education system and Sikhism focuses on patriotism as the aim of education.

• **Political ideologies:** Political ideologies certainly have a say in determining educational aims. The educational aims of a democratic political system can be quite different from that of an autocratic political set-up.

• **Socioeconomic factors:** These factors play an important role affecting the aims of education. The social system, social ideology and economy of a country are important factors to affect the aims of education. • Cultural factors: Education plays an important role in transmitting cultural heritage and traditionsfrom one generation to another. Culture also develops educational aims by itself.

• **Intellectual factors:** As education is fully scientific today, it has to aim at exploring new information and knowledge. from one generation to another. Culture also develops educational aims by itself.

• **Intellectual factors:** As education is fully scientific today, it has to aim at exploring new information and knowledge.

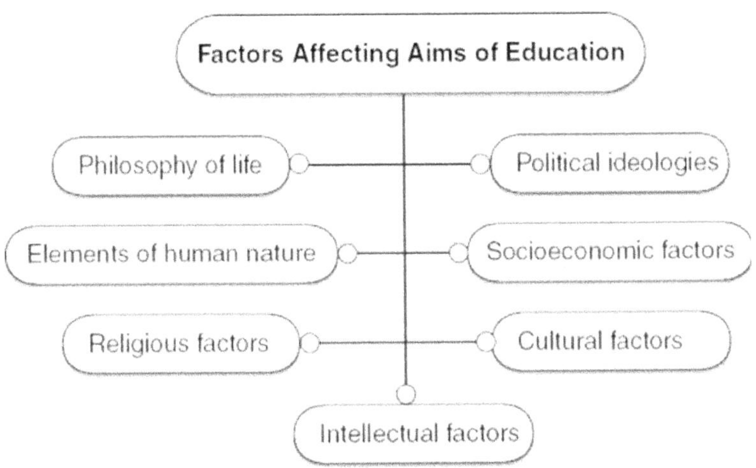

Q 5. Definition of learning.

= Teaching and learning activities are twin activities involved in the total educational process. Teaching and learning are closely related and they are reciprocal to each other. Teaching cannot be thought without an idea of learning and learning is not possible without teaching activities.

Any activity can be called learning so far as it develops the individual and makes his/her behavior and experiences different from what that would otherwise have been. —Woodworth R.S.

Learning is a process that results in the modification of behavior. —J.F. Travers

Learning may be considered as a change in insights, behavior, perception, motivation or a combination of these. —M.L. Bigge

Learning is the process by which behavior is originated or changes through practice and training. —Kingsley H.L. and Garry R.

Q6 .Characteristics of learning.

= Any activity can be called learning so far as it develops the individual and makes his/her behavior and experiences different from what that would otherwise have been. —Woodworth R.S.

Learning is a process that results in the modification of behavior. —J.F. Travers

Learning may be considered as a change in insights, behavior, perception, motivation or a combination of these. —M.L. Bigge

Learning is the process by which behavior is originated or changes t

=. Characteristics of learning Learning is the acquisition of knowledge and/or skill through education and experience. Our ability to learn and our intellectual capacity are intangibles.

Detailed discussion about the characteristics of learning is given below .

• Learning is unitary: The process of learning helps the learner respond as a whole person in a unified way to the whole situation or total pattern. He responds intellectually, emotionally, spiritually and physically and these occur simultaneously. He reacts to the whole learning situation rather than to any single stimulus.

• Learning is individual and social: Learning is in a sense an entirely individual matter. Each individual must learn his or her own activity. In a larger sense, all learning is social, as it takes place in response to the environment in which there are other individuals as well as physical things. Learning is social because it takes place as a type of response to an individual's social environment. It is important that each person do his or her own learning irrespective of their individual differences, their capacities and level of intelligence.

• Learning is purposive: Learning is not only active but active in a specific direction. It helps the individuals achieve goals or purposes in their life. Learning cannot be meaningful and efficacious without persistent selective and purposeful effort.

Learning not only contributes to an individual's purposes at times but enables him/her to make more intelligent adjustments in future.

• Learning is creative: Human learning is both selective and creative. Man is the only creature on earth who is not merely a creature but a creator as well. Learning helps a man to be more creative in life. It is the process of personal choice making. Learning helps him be creative for the betterment of the society.

Learning modifies the behaviour of the individual: Learning affects the conduct of the individual. True learning takes place only when the individual acquires a type of knowledge or a skill that changes his or her attitudes and appreciations in response to a real need and modifies his or her conduct in accordance with new learning and therefore is changed.

• Learning helps in the organization of experiences: The process of learning is not mere acquisition of facts and skills through drill and repetition. It involves organization and evaluation of learning materials. The learner reorganizes his or her experience and behaviour.

• Learning helps make choices in life: Change is a law of nature and things are changing around us in the universe at every movement. Therefore, learning is as essential as food and physical exercise so that one can make wise decisions and adaptations with the changes one witnesses in his surroundings. Thus it will not be wrong to state that changes as well as learning are lifelong processes because as changes in life take place every day, learning is also needed every moment to make best choices and decisions in life.

• Learning helps bring changes in life: Everyone of us needs change and progress in life; however questions arise on how one can achieve fast and prompt changes and progress in life. The answer is learning, because when one acquires new knowledge he/she tries to apply it on the ground that ultimately brings about change and progress in life. All rapid changes and human progress in the world is the result of new learning.

• Learning helps in continuous professional development: Learning does not end at the completion of a particular course or educational programme but is needed throughout life for continuous professional development of the individual. For example, health care professionals including nurses regularly engage in professional education such as seminars, symposiums, workshops and conferences essential for their continuous professional development.

- Learning helps keep in tune with trends and development in particular fields: Learning provides an individual, a new way of thinking and professionals must acquire new knowledge to meet the pace with emerging new demands of their consumers. For example, India is catching up with medical tourism; nurses and health care professionals have to equip themselves with the emerging health care demands of these new health care consumers. Learning helps such individuals be in tune with new trends and development of their profession.

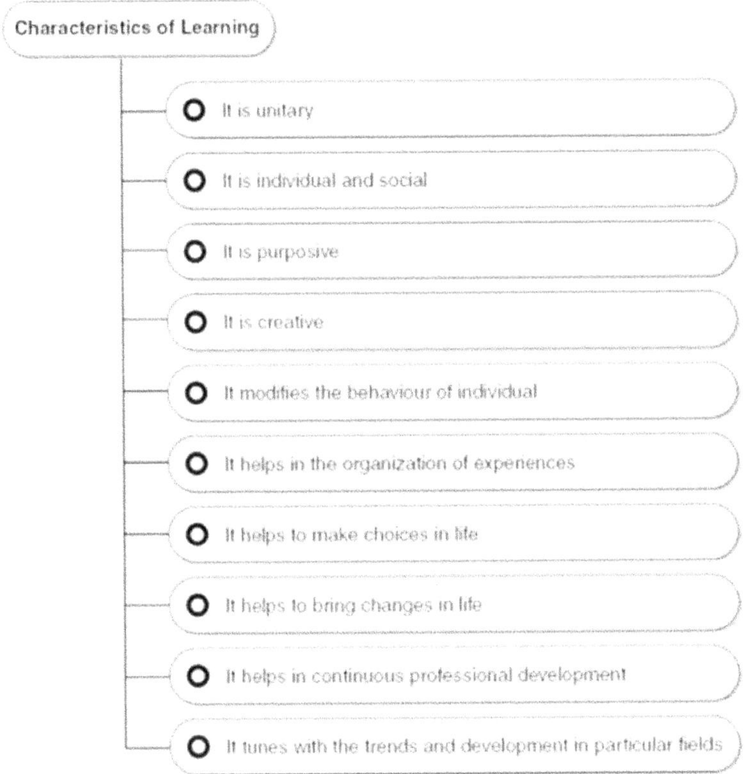

Q 7. Principles of learning

= Any activity can be called learning so far as it develops the individual and makes his/her behavior and experiences different from what that would otherwise have been. —Woodworth R.S.

Learning is a process that results in the modification of behavior. —J.F. Travers

Learning may be considered as a change in insights, behavior, perception, motivation or a combination of these. —M.L. Bigge

Learning is the process by which behavior is originated or changes t

PRINCIPLES OF LEARNING

Basic fundamental principles of learning

Learning is

- motivated by adjustment with new things
- universal in nature
- never-ending growth
- a continuous process
- goal directed or purposive
- active and creative
- aroused by individual and social needs
- response of the whole individual to the total situation
- transferable
- possible on cognitive, affective and conative side
- a process not a product
- Learning brings progressive change in behaviour of learner

The main principles of learning are discussed below.

- **Brings progressive change in behaviour:** Learning brings progressive change in behaviour as the individual reacts to situations and this is how learning leads to improvement in an individual.
- **Learning is motivated by adjustment:** The individual has to adjust to the new environment.

Learning is universal in nature: Man is a rational animal and learns more than other animals from nature; however learning does occur in other animals, since it is an omnipresent phenomenon.

- **Learning is never-ending growth:** Every individual has an inspiration to learn more. One achievement leads to further incentive, pursuit and effort. Therefore, learning is the never-ending growing phenomenon of an individual.
- **Learning is a continuous process**: Learning is continuous and not restricted to the childhood but grows with life. Death is the end of learning.

• **Learning is goal directed or purposive**: When the purpose or goal of learning is clear, vivid and explicit, learning becomes meaningful and effective to the learner.

• **Learning is active and creative:** Learning largely depends on the activities of a learner. It is said no learning can take place where there is no self activity. Learning results from the activity and experience. • Learning is aroused by individual and social needs: Learning depends on individuals: their needs, problems, interests, attitudes, ambitions and needs of the society. Learning may be quick and fast for some individuals and in others it may be slow or steady. No learning can take place in the absence of social environment.

Learning is transferable: Learning is a transferable phenomenon, which may transfer from one learning generation to the next generation learners. A transfer of learning content may take place but the amount of transfer may vary from situation to situation and from individual to individual. Transfer occurs when there is similarity of content, techniques, ideals, procedures, interest and attitudes.

Learning is a process not a product: Learning is an ongoing process as it goes on and on and is a never-ending process; death of an individual is considered as the end point of learning. Therefore, it is considered a lifelong process rather than an end product of a particular point of life.

Q 8. Factors influencing learning .

= Any activity can be called learning so far as it develops the individual and makes his/her behavior and experiences different from what that would otherwise have been. —Woodworth R.S.

Learning is a process that results in the modification of behavior. —J.F. Travers

Learning may be considered as a change in insights, behavior, perception, motivation or a combination of these. —M.L. Bigge

Learning is the process by which behavior is originated or changes t

Factors influencing learning are classified under two main headings: intrinsic and extrinsic factors (Fig. Details of the intrinsic and extrinsic factors influencing learning are given below.

I. Intrinsic factors

Intrinsic factors are from within the individual learner such as age, intelligence, attention, interest, holistic health, maturation, fatigue, insight, ability, capacity and motivation.

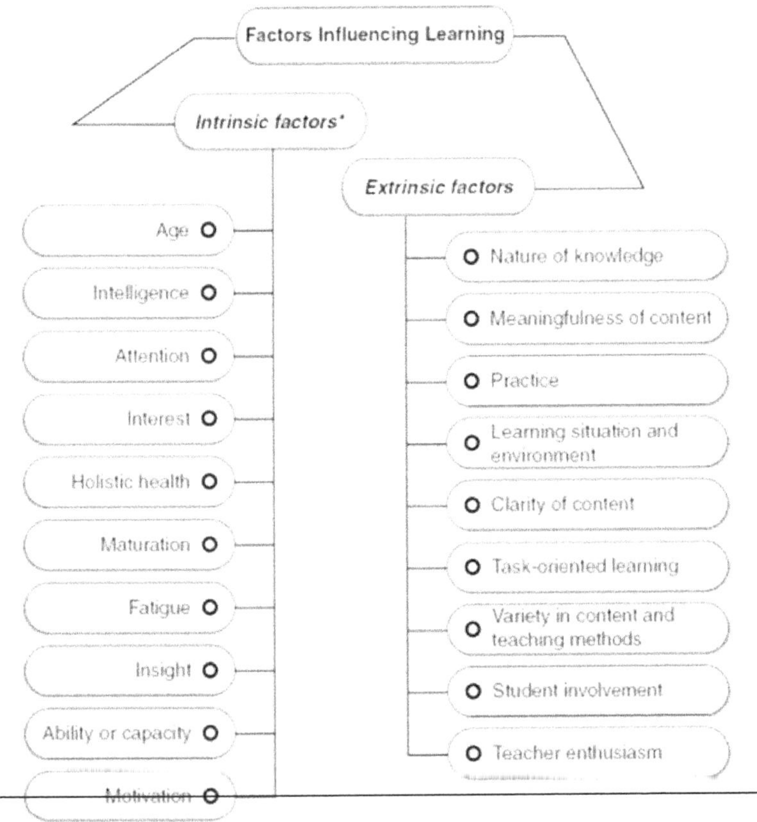

• Age: Age can impact the capability to learn. A child can learn faster and an aged person will have difficulty learning the modern ways of knowledge.

Intelligence: Mental ability of an individual can affect learning. Individuals with subaverage intelligence will learn later than individuals with normal intelligence level.

• Attention: Attention plays an important role in the education and training process. Attention is not static. It fluctuates from one object to another. Inattention by trainees is responsible for poor learning.

• Interest: Interest is an inner disposition or a tendency of readiness to perceive. Effective learning requires assimilation and interest. Interest should be aroused before learning begins and for satisfactory results it should be maintained throughout the learning period.

• Holistic health: Physical and intellectual health promotes effective learning. Without sound intellectual or physical health, an individual is unable to fulfil the demands of the learning process.

• Maturation: Learning depends on intellectual age. Maturation means intellectual, social maturity and psychological readiness. The changes associated with normal growth are called maturation.

• Fatigue: Every physical activity involves the consumption of energy. Human efficiency is the ratio between achievement and energy spent. Mental fatigue is caused by a loss of interest and the monotonous nature of work. When an individual is tired

He/she cannot pay attention or concentrate towards learning activities.

• Insight: Insight also plays an important part in learning. Without clear insight it is impossible to achieve predetermined goals of learning. Insight is based on the ability of synthesizing the perceived facts and factors. It involves creative and imaginative thinking.

• Ability or capacity: Different species of animals have a different capacity to learn. Man is known to have a greater capacity to learn than other living beings. Even men vary in their ability to learn.

• Motivation: Motivation is a general term that encompasses the states of the individual under which he attends to certain aspects of his environment. As a result, his behaviour is both initiated and directed.

I. **Extrinsic factors**

Extrinsic factors are from outside the individual learner and interfere directly or indirectly with an individual's learning process such as nature of knowledge, meaningfulness of content, practice, learning situation and environment, clarity of content, task-oriented learning, verity in content and teaching methods, student involvement and teacher enthusiasm.

• **Nature of knowledge**: If knowledge is interesting in nature, an individual can learn it more efficiently.

• **Meaningfulness of content:** Meaningless material can neither be learnt easily nor kept in memory for the long term. If the material is meaningful, the individual will learn it more effectively and easily.

• **Practice:** Practice, exercise, repetition or drill are interchangeable terms that are presumed to have something to do with learning. Simple acts are learnt in single trials, but complex acts are learnt through exercises or repeated trials.

• **Learning situation and environment**: A learner should have a conducive environment to learn that will promote the learning process. For example, adequate ventilation, lighting, temperature, odour free environment, absence of nose disturbance, rodent and insect free environment and availability of good library resources.

• **Clarity of content:** Clarity is the ability of the learner to clearly see, hear and understand what is being said. Threats to clarity include small fonts, slurred speech, obstructions to sight and ambiguous language.

- **Task-orientated learning:** People tend to learn better when they are engaged in tasks.
- **Variety in content and teaching methods**: A variety of ways used by the teacher can enhance the students' learning. Some people learn by listening, some by seeing and some by doing.
- **Student involvement:** Student involvement in the whole teaching–learning process is very crucial for his or her learning. Active involvement of students not only motivates them but also arouses interest in particular activities.
- **Teacher enthusiasm**: Enthusiasm of the teachers or presenters is contagious. If the teacher shows interest in a topic, the learners are more likely to be interested..

Q 8 Nature of learning

= Any activity can be called learning so far as it develops the individual **and** makes his/her behavior and experiences different from what that would otherwise have been. —Woodworth R.S.

Learning is a process that results in the modification of behavior. —J.F. Travers

Learning may be considered as a change in insights, behavior, perception, motivation or a combination of these. —M.L. Bigge

Learning is the process by which behavior is originated or changes t

Following are some of the significant views about the nature of learning:

- **Behaviourist view:** Learning is a change in behaviour as a result of experience. Men and other living beings react to the environment.
- **Gestalt view:** According to this view, learning depends on gestalt or configuration (wholeness of the situation). Learning is a total reaction to the total situation.
- **Hormic view:** This view was developed by McDougall. It stresses on the purposeful nature of learning, i.e. learning is a goal-

directed activity.

• **Trial and error view:** This view was put forward by Thorndike. He conducted many experiments on dogs, cats and fish and concluded that most learning takes place by trial and error.

Q.11. Explain the method of learning / Process of learning.

= Any activity can be called learning so far as it develops the individual and makes his/her behavior and experiences different from what that would otherwise have been. —Woodworth R.S.

Learning is a process that results in the modification of behavior. —J.F. Travers

Learning may be considered as a change in insights, behavior, perception, motivation or a combination of these. —M.L. Bigge

Learning is a process which involves a series of steps

• Motive of the learner: Motive or need arises first. Motive is the force that impinges or compels the individual to behave or react or do a particular task.

• Establishing goals: If a motive or need is present, the goal is set up by the teacher and learner.

• Teacher–student adjustment: Adjustment on the part of the students and teacher to each other and the environment

. • Change in the student's behavior : During this phase, inappropriate behaviours are dropped and new behaviours are acquired by the student. Changes in behaviour in an individual take place after due interaction of the student with the educational environment and/or teacher.

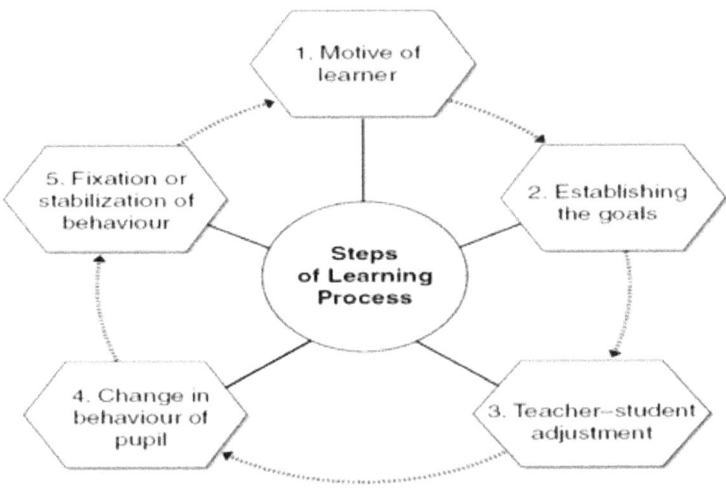

FIGURE 6.2 Learning process.

Fixation or stabilization of behaviour: Later the changes in the behaviour of the learner acquainted are expected to be fixed and stabilized for permanence..

Q 12 . Enlist relationship between teaching and learning .

= Any activity can be called learning so far as it develops the individual and makes his/her behavior and cxpcricnccs different from what that would otherwise have been. —Woodworth R.S.

Learning is a process that results in the modification of behavior. —J.F. Travers

Learning may be considered as a change in insights, behavior, perception, motivation or a combination of these. —M.L. Bigge

RELATIONSHIP BETWEEN TEACHING & LEARNING

1. Both teaching & learning may be formal or informal.
2. Both are goal oriented.
3. Good teaching results in good learning.
4. One can observe teaching but not learning.
5. Both teaching and learning require skills, creativity, intelligence and operate on definite principles.
6. Good teaching requires good communication skill & good learning requires good listening skills.
7. Only good learners become good teachers.

Relationship Between Teaching and Learning

The most important moments in teaching and learning is how the teacher teaches and how the learner learn. What is responsible for those few moments. The best college course and teachers so involve students that they learn as much as they can think about the subject out side the classroom. Moreover instructors who are motivated by their subject ... foster students interest by personal examples. Teacher's interest infects lectures and discussion and can spread the student's work out side the class.

Relationship Between Teaching and Learning

When teacher cannot make student learn, they can promote learning by helping students become motivated to learn, handle information and experience, develop knowledge, attitude and skill and transfer their learning from classroom to real world. In addition to the general role of the teacher as helper, literature on the relationship between teaching learning identifies three specific roles.

Relationship Between Teaching and Learning

The teacher as human relations specialistThe teacher as facilitator andThe teacher as motivator

Relationship Between Teaching and Learning

Learning is infused with the complexity of learners' lives. A variety of different factors are interrelated and integrated in the learning-teaching process. Learning is therefore not predictable as a product of input, but created through constant negotiations between individuals, social environments and broader social influences.Teachers and researchers need to pay attention to the beliefs about learning, teaching, language and literacy which learners and teachers bring with them to the learning-teaching encounter. Beliefs also shape curricula and teaching materials. There are likely to be matches and mismatches among these beliefs.

Relationship Between Teaching and Learning

Both teachers and learners come to class with purposes and goal. Teachers and researchers should identify participants' purpose as a key factor in learning events.A full understanding of learning in adult must take account of social aspects of learning, including the political and institutional context in which it takes place, the broader socio-cultural context in which learning is situated, and the social life in classrooms.

Relationship Between Teaching and Learning

Social interaction is the key mechanism through which learning takes place. Its characteristics need to be studied in detail as a means to understanding the dynamics whereby teaching can facilitate learning.Teaching is best characterized as the creation of 'learning opportunities' through the management of interaction. The concept of 'learning opportunities' accounts for the way in which different learners learn different things from the same learning-teaching event, and provides a rationale for approaches to teaching which do not attempt to specify exactly what is to be learned.

Relationship Between Teaching and Learning

There are several different types of potential outcome from learning-teaching events: learning about content, learning how to learn, learning about language, learning about social relations, re-constructing identities, and wider benefits of learning such as increased self-assurance. Researchers and teachers should seek to establish learners' perceptions and interpretations of teaching learning events.

Relationship Between Teaching and Learning

Rather than trying to make generalizations about particular

teaching methods, it is more useful to try to understand how learning opportunities and possible outcomes emerge in particular contexts. For the process to be meaningful, learners' other languages and/or interpreters need to be used.

Q 13. Maxims of teaching

= Maxims of teaching

The maxims of teaching may be defined as rules for presenting difficult terms and concepts to make them easy to comprehend in classroom teaching. A teacher employs some specific ways to organize teaching to make the terms and concepts communicable up to the cognition or rational process and level of learners. They are the guidelines for teaching. The maxims of teaching are very helpful in obtaining the active involvement and participation of learners in the teaching–learning process. They quicken the interest of the learners and motivate them to learn. They make students attentive to the teaching–learning process.

I. **Features of maxims of teaching**

- Maxim helps in organizing teaching–learning activities.
- It makes presentation of terms and concepts easily understandable.
- It enables teacher to make his communication for the mental level of the students.
- It is an important component of instructional procedure which is used in designing and presenting content in effective way.

II. Essential maxims of teaching Following are some of the essential maxims of teaching :

- **From simple to complex or easy to difficult:** The nature of this maxim is more psychological that a child learns easy things and then proceeds towards complex things. For example, initially nursing students are taught about basic care procedures and then about complex procedures such as electrocardiogram (ECG) and central venous pressure (CVP) monitoring.

• **From known to unknown:** This maxim is based on the appreciative mass theory of learning. It assumes that student-acquired knowledge is given by linking with actuarial knowledge so the student can learn better and retain for a longer time. Students have some knowledge and teachers should enlarge this knowledge. If we link new knowledge with the old knowledge we can make teaching clearer and effective. This maxim makes a link between the old and the new. If the teacher does not follow this maxim, then it is possible that students may be confused and may be interested in learning.

• **From part to whole**: B.F. Skinner gives emphasis on the part to whole maxim of teaching. He assumes that a student learns well if content is presented in small parts.

• **From whole to part**: According to the Gestalt school of psychology, whole is more important than parts. The whole is more motivating, understandable and effective than the study of various parts. A teacher should organize his activities in such a way that students can perceive the whole and then its parts because the whole attracts first. For example, while teaching chambers of heart, the teacher should show the entire heart first and then proceed with teaching the structure and functions of each part of the heart.

• **Proceed from concrete to abstract**: This is also a psychological rule of learning. Herbert said 'our lessons should start from the concrete and end in abstract'. A child's imagination is greatly aided by concrete material. 'Things first and words after' is a common saying. Rousseau said, 'things, things and things'. Children cannot think in abstractions in the beginning. Young children learn first from the things they can see and handle. Students learn from perception and experience about objects. After perception, concepts which are partially concrete and partially abstract in nature are formed.

• **From particular to general**: Particular facts are easy to understand as compared to general facts. Particular facts and examples should be presented to the children before giving them general rules and principles. Particular is an inductive method and general is a deductive method. The process of induction is easier to comprehend than the so-called deductive one.

- **From analysis to synthesis:** Analysis and synthesis both are intellectual processes. This maxim is most frequently used in creative teaching. Analysis is an intellectual process. When a student comes to school, his knowledge is incomplete, indefinite and imperfect. Analysis makes the student's incomplete, indefinite and incoherent knowledge complete, definite and coherent. A teacher should begin teaching with analysis, so that complex problems are divided into systematic and comprehensible units. Synthesis must be performed in the end to make the knowledge definite and fixed. Analysis is useful for understanding and synthesis is useful for fixing this knowledge in students' minds.
- **From empirical to rational:** Empirical knowledge is based on the observations of students and has a significant role in a student's learning process. A student acquires most of his learning through observations. Learning by imitation is also based on observation. The activities of the teacher should be so organized that they can provide new experiences through observation and the teacher should then proceed with the logical aspect.
- **From psychological to logical:** The psychological approach takes into consideration student interests, abilities, aptitude, developmental level, needs and reactions. Logical approach considers the subject matter and its arrangement into logical steps and orders. An eminent writer remarked, 'logical procedure has its place in the middle of a lesson but the approach must be determined psychologically'. First, the teachers should keep in mind the selection of the subject matter to be presented. After this, the teachers should have a logical approach to arrange the matter into logical orders and steps.
- **From actual to representative:** The child learns more easily and quickly from actual, natural and real objects rather than from representative objects like models, charts and other aids. For example, while learning about a milk plant, an actual visit to the milk plant will make the learning more vivid and rapid rather than

from a picture or model.

- **From induction to deduction**: Induction means drawing a conclusion from a set of examples. The process of induction calls for perception, reasoning, judgement and generalization. The teacher should proceed from induction to deduction, i.e. first present the principle or generalization before students and then verify the truth of this principle by applying it to particular instances. Induction discovers knowledge and deduction is the consequence of such discoveries.
- **From general to specific**: Explain general rules first and then specific ones. For example, while teaching paediatric nursing, the teacher explains the principles of paediatric nursing and then teaches about various disease conditions and the procedures related to child health.
- **From specific to general**: In certain situations, it is imperative to proceed from specific to general. For example, the role of iron in the body has to be specified before generalizing the consequences of anaemia on the body.
- **From indefinite to definite**: The ideas of students in initial stages are vague. These ideas should be made definite, clear, precise and systematic by adopting effective teaching methods. To make these ideas definite, the teacher can use audiovisual aids and other strategies as needed.
- **Proceed from overview to details:** Students can easily comprehend if the teacher proceeds from an overview to details. For example, while teaching about the instruments used for performing an endoscopy, the teacher should introduce all instruments by listing down their names before explaining their uses and the ways to handle each instrument in detail.
- **From observation to reasoning:** The teacher has to provide an opportunity for the students to see and notice the factors involved in a particular topic or context before explaining the reasons associated with it or eliciting reasons from the students.
- **To follow nature:** This maxim of teaching is based on the philosophy of naturalism. Rousseau has given the concept to follow

nature. The child is the centre of educational processes. A child should be given full freedom to learn according to his own ways. The teacher's role is to observe his behaviour and learning activities. There should be one teacher and one student in an ideal situation.

CHAPTER SIX

METHODS OF TEACHING

SHORT ANSWER

Q 1. Enlist the various methods of teaching.

=

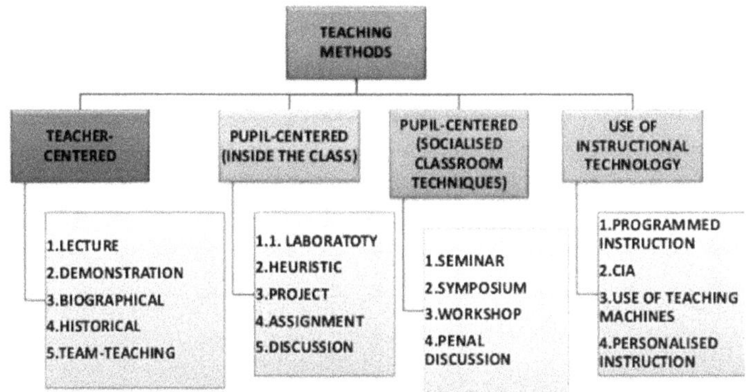

Teacher centered :

1 . LECTURE METHOD

Introduction

The lecture is one of the most well-known, highly effective teaching method, through which some educational purposes are well served. The lecture, when it is adjusted to stimulate and organize thinking, active learning.

Definition

"The lecture is essentially a formal exposition, which makes only incidental use of narrative description setting forth the basic and all inclusive structure of an entire topic".

Purposes

Stimulates process of thinking among teachers and learners

Teacher will gain teaching skills and learn how to attack a problem in a systematic way

2 . TEAM TEACHING

Definitions

A method of coordinated classroom teaching which involves a team of teachers working together with a single group of students " .

An arrangement whereby 2 or more teachers , with or without teaching aides cooperatively plan , instruct , and evaluate one or more class groups in an appropriate instructional space and given length of time so as to take advantage of the special competencies of the team members " .

Pupil – Centered : (inside Class Room)

1 . Exhibition

Exhibition are familiar items in our environment today. When we go round an exhibition, our attention is often focused on a group of objects and materials that are displayed according to a deliberate plan.

2 . ASSIGNMENT METHOD

a personally advocated for teaching different subjects to learners in the higher classes . The syllabus is split o significant units of topics . Each unit or topic , in its turn is subdivided into learning assignments for learners . The learners are usually required to prepare the assignments in writing . Written assignments help in organization of knowledge , assimilation of facts and better preparation for examinations

Pupil – Centered (Socialized class room techniques) :

1 . Seminar

MEANING:

1. A meeting for discussion or training.

2. Group of student meeting together to discuss topic with teacher

3. Group of supervised students doing research or advanced study.

DEFINITION:

Seminar is a group of members come together to exchange views of current problems of to share with others their own experiences, experiments, discoveries etc.

2 . **Symposium**

Symposium is a type of socialized technique whereas each of participants is expected to present a well reasoned argument or point of view with respect to the problem being discussed.

MEANING: Syn- together Posis- a drinking

1. A drinking parting at which there was intellectual conversation.

2. Any meeting or social gathering at which ideas are freely exchanged.

DEFINITION: Symposium is a method of group discussion in which two or more persons under the direction of chairman present separate speeches which gives several aspects of one question.

MEMBERS INVOLVED IN SYMPOSIUM: 1. Chairman 2. Speaker 3. Audience

3 . Panel discussion

Panel disscussion is discussion in which 4 to 8 qualified personnel sit and discuss the topic in front of large group or audience. Panel discussion has a chairperson (moderator) and 4 to 8 speakers. The success of the panel discussion depends upon the chairperson. He is the one who has to keep the discussion going and develop train of thought.

Use of Instructional technology

Programmed Instruction

A Programme is a device to control the student's behavior and help them to learn without the direct supervision of a teacher. Instruction is the purposeful, orderly, controlled sequencing of experiences, to reach a specified goal.

Programmed Instruction is the presentation of material in a step by step procedure with knowledge of results and the possibility of different courses through instruction. Burrhus Frederic Skinner

field trip

Direct experience with reality provides an excellent opportunity for sensory learning, field trip is a first audio- visual aid to be introduced in audio- visual media for effective learning. The specific advantage of field trip is that after the trip students just say, I have seen, instead of I have read about or I have been told.

Q 2. Explain principles of teaching.

= **Principles of teaching**

Teaching principles help teachers develop an insight regarding their strengths and weaknesses and provide information pertaining to teaching like:

- Whom to teach?
- Why to teach?
- Where to teach?
- What to teach?
- How to teach?
- When to teach?

The principles of teaching are discussed under two subheadings: general and psychological principles

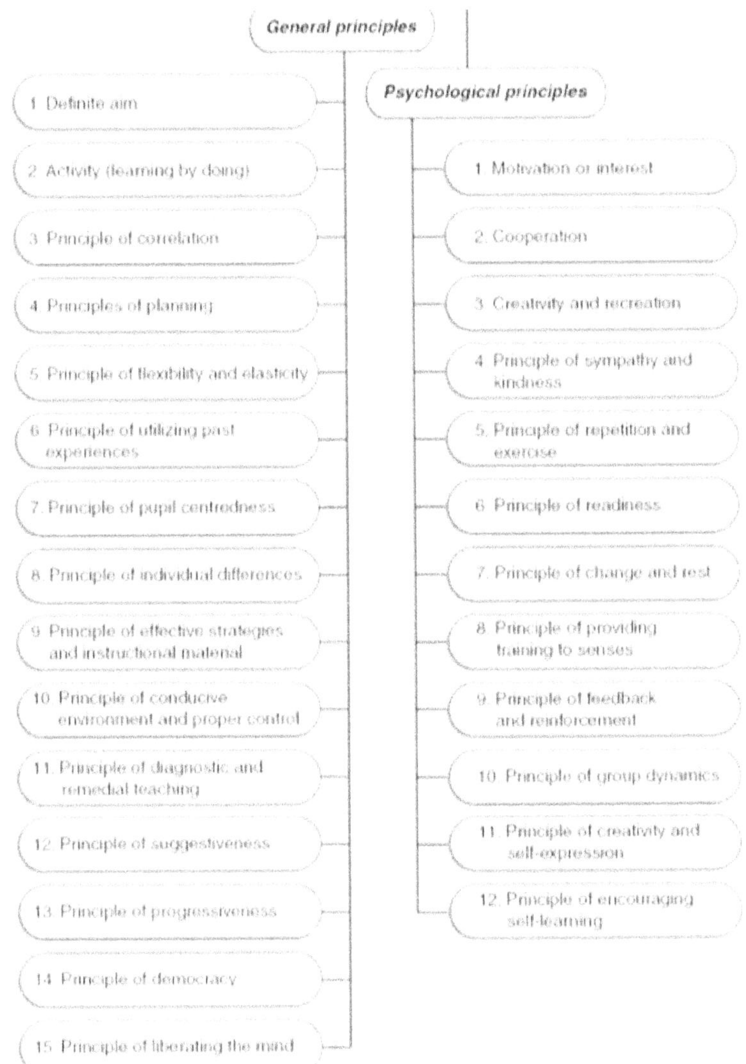

General principles of teaching

- **Definite aim:** Teaching should start with a definite aim that is of great help to both the teacher and the student. It makes the teaching and learning interesting, effective, precise and definite. Without definite aim the teacher might go astray and his teaching might lack coherence and definiteness. The students do not gain much if the lesson plan is haphazardly and aimlessly planned. Without definite aim, even the best lesson would fail to achieve its objectives.

- **Activity (learning by doing):** Teaching is effective when students actively participate in the lesson. Learning becomes active and quicker if the student is physically as well as mentally active. Students learn through self activity but the activity must be psychologically sound. Learning by doing removes the dullness of the lesson and puts children in life situations. The child engages himself fully and learns qualitatively as well as quantitatively. Teaching should be organized to provide the child with the maximum opportunity to learn by doing.
- **Principle of correlation (linking with actual life and other subjects):** Life and learning should become two poles of the same magnet; they are interdependent and cannot exist without one another. The teacher should not teach in water-tight compartments. Good teaching implies that learning must be vitally linked with the life of the learners and other subjects of their syllabus. For example, before teaching a topic in medical–surgical nursing, one must correlate it with the basic anatomy and physiology of a particular system.
- **Principles of planning:** The success of the teaching–learning process is directly proportional to planning. Successful teaching is always well planned. Planning involves selection, division and revision.
- **Selection:** The teaching material should be carefully selected. The teaching material should be selected according to the instructional objectives, the teacher's ability to impart knowledge and the learner's capacity to digest the subject matter.
- **Division:** Division makes breaking the chosen subject matter into convenient and meaningful units to make it more understandable. The technique of dividing the subject into units

and subunits facilitates the teaching–learning process.

- **Revision:** Drill and practice are essential for the assimilation of knowledge. Revision helps assimilation and helps the teacher to test the understanding of his students.
- **Principle of flexibility and elasticity:** Teaching should not be rigid and stereotyped. It should be flexible and elastic. The teacher should be resourceful, original, imaginative and creative enough to adapt himself to the requirements of the students and the teaching–learning situation.
- **Principle of utilizing past experiences:** New knowledge can be acquired on the basis of past experiences. Teaching should be linked with already acquired knowledge and experiences. It facilitates teaching and helps achieve the stipulated objectives with great ease and economy.
- **Principle of pupil centredness:** Teaching should be pupil centred, i.e. the needs, interests, abilities, aspirations of the students should be given due importance in teaching.
- **Principle of individual differences:** No two individuals are alike. They differ in their attitudes, abilities, interests, achievements, aims, ambitions and aspirations. Some are slow learners and some are quick learners. Good teaching always respects the individuality of students. By considering each student as a unique individual, the teacher can pay attention to individual differences and develop strategies to cater to the educational needs of the individual student.
- **Principle of effective strategies and instructional material:** The teacher must take care to choose appropriate strategies, devices and instructional material for teaching a particular topic/subject. For example, to teach foetal circulation, the teacher can use diagrams or live videos to make teaching more effective
- . **Principle of conducive environment and proper control:** Conducive environment and proper control facilitate teaching and learning. Various factors can affect the teaching–learning process such as teacher, principal, teacher–teacher, principal–teacher and pupil–teacher relationship, group dynamics, classroom interaction,

discipline, room temperature, light, ventilation, cleanliness and seating arrangement.

- **Principle of diagnostic and remedial teaching**: In successful teaching, it is necessary that a teacher should know the difficulties and problems of the students with a view to remove them. Successful teacher is that who is able to remove the difficulties of the students and solve their problems.
- **Principle of suggestiveness:** Good teaching proceeds on the basis of suggestion rather than direction. The teacher suggests activities, materials and modes of responses. Suggestions help in securing cooperation of the pupils. Good teachers give suggestions instead of giving orders.
- **Principle of progressiveness:** The ultimate aim of the education is overall development and progress of the child. Therefore, good teaching always strives for progressiveness of the child towards development of skills, abilities, attitude and interest in essential domain of personal and professional life.
- **Principle of democracy:** Each individual is entitled to equal rights. The teacher should create a democratic environment in the class. Students should not be taught with their caste, creed or religion in mind.
- **Principle of liberating the mind:** The ideal of good teaching is to liberate the mind of students from any fear, which he may incidentally feel and to develop independence in thought and method of procedure so that he may be able to solve his problems independently and work out solutions.

Psychological principles of teaching

- **Motivation or interest**: Teaching is directed towards promoting learning through motivating the learner or creating an interest in learning. Motivation is the key to the success of learning. Furthermore, motivation is like a petrol engine that drives the psychological engine. The teacher should properly motivate the students by creating interesting learning situations.
- **Cooperation:** Teaching is a cooperative affair between the teacher and the students. Poor cooperation leads to a poor

teaching–learning process.

• **Creativity and recreation**: Teaching is not to be continued as a routine affair, but should arouse creativeness in the child. A sense of creativeness brings interest and pleasure in learning among learners, which ultimately leads to effective learning. Good teaching must strive to bring creativeness and a sense of recreation in the learners.

• **Principle of sympathy and kindness:** Successful teaching cannot take place in a situation that lacks sympathy and kindness with the interests and needs of the students. Students learn more when they are taught in a kind and polite manner.

• **Principle of repetition and exercise:** 'Practice makes a man perfect' is a well-known proverb. It applies well to the field of teaching and learning. If students are asked to repeat learning tasks, they will understand, retain and recall the subject matter more effectively.

• **Principle of readiness:** If students are not ready to learn, it is the teacher's duty to make them ready for learning. Teachers can choose the teaching tasks according to the student's psychology, i.e. their abilities, interests, attitudes, aspirations, maturation and development level.

• **Principle of change and rest:** Monotony fatigue and lack of attention decreases the speed of learning. Teaching–learning process followed by rest and change refreshes the mind and prepares the learners for more and effective learning.

• **Principle of providing training to senses**: Senses are gateways of knowledge. The power of observation, identification, discrimination, experimentation, application and generalization can be developed through proper training and functioning of the senses. The teacher should make proper arrangements for training the senses especially the senses of sight and hearing.

• **Principle of feedback and reinforcement**: Feedback about the progress of the student and further reinforcement are the most essential components of the teaching–learning process. Students are motivated for effective learning through timely and effective feedback and reinforcement.

- **Principle of group dynamics:** Group dynamics plays an important role in achievement of teaching objectives. Students tend to learn better in a group and also develop qualities of cooperation, mutual respect, sacrifice, etc. Therefore, the teacher should encourage group learning.
- **Principle of creativity and self-expression:** The development of the society and nation depends on creative ideas. It becomes imperative that the teacher should create situations in a classroom that inculcate creativity and self-expression in students. Usually, teachers feel happy if the students reproduce the same material in exactly the same manner. This practice can hinder a student's development and needs to be discouraged.
- **Principle of encouraging self-learning:** The teacher should inculcate habits of self-study, independent work and self-learning in the students by providing students with opportunities and training for this purpose.

Q 3 .Explain in detail about lecture method.

= **Introduction**

The lecture is one of the most well-known, highly effective teaching method, through which some educational purposes are well served. The lecture, when it is adjusted to stimulate and organize thinking, active learning.

Definition

"The lecture is essentially a formal exposition, which makes only incidental use of narrative description setting forth the basic and all inclusive structure of an entire topic".

Purposes

Stimulates process of thinking among teachers and learners

Teacher will gain teaching skills and learn how to attack a problem in a systematic way .

Expertise teaching skills are necessary to make teaching effective and facilitate Learning , to teach varied subjects for a larger group of students , lecture method is ideal

Good teacher with efficient teaching skills and vast subject knowledge is always beneficial for the students as those teachers will be role models for the learners throughout their life time . A good teacher is an asset an organization.

A lesson taught by an effective teacher always beneficial than several hours of independence studying or unlimited group discussions .

A teacher opens a topic in a field of study , draw attention to a group of students to its vital elements ,extract the essential , bring students abreast of development in the forefront of Research .

The lecture should illuminate , supplement and reinforce the topic being studied , the teacher has to do vast review of the content and thoroughly prepare about a specific topic in advance , formulate a lesson plan and plans the method of teaching quite ahead of time . The lecture should not be a mere representation of exactly what is in the text books nor assigned reading , nor it should be completely unrelated to the subject topic . The teacher should be very careful while teaching to the group of students by whatever method of teaching they adopt .

• Teacher will illustrate with suitable examples from other related sources , out of their professional experience as it enhances students ' thinking and understanding the subject effectively and promotes long lasting learning with a factual basis with relevant concepts , practices the same principles wherever it is applicable .

A well prepared lecture will be more beneficial for the students to have organized knowledge in an integrating fashion as the student uses cross references , correlates lecture material with other resources.

• Teacher will be exemplify the techniques of analysis in a field of study by using scientific principles The teacher can introduce an organizing content in presentation , involves the student with appropriate teaching learning activities , make the students in arriving at the generalizations and conclusions .

Teacher creates interest and enthusiasm in the subject , promotes respect in students mind for the ides worth whileness of intellectual values through their mode of presentation and instructional material .

Q 4 . Advantages and disadvantages of lecture method .

= The lecture is one of the most well-known, highly effective teaching method, through which some educational purposes are well served. The lecture, when it is adjusted to stimulate and organize thinking, active learning.

Definition

"The lecture is essentially a formal exposition, which makes only incidental use of narrative description setting forth the basic and all inclusive structure of an entire topic".

Advantage of lecture methods

- Factual information
- Useful for large gathering
- Cost effective
- Quick and straight forward way
- Useful methods for auditory learner
- Easier to create
- Familiar methods
- Time saving

Disadvantage of lecture methods

- Content centered
- One sided affair
- Need proficient oral skills- teacher need special oral skill in delivering lecture. If they don't have this skill then lecture become boring, and uninteresting.
- Passive audience
- Minimizes feedback from students.

Q 5. Microteaching .

= MICROTEACHING

Introduction

A training procedure aimed at simplifying the complexities of the regular teaching process . The trainee is engaged in a scaled - down teaching situation . Scaled down in terms of class size (small group 4-6 learners . length of class time (5 to 10 minutes) , teaching tasks (practicing and mastering of a specific teaching skill . eg lecturing , questioning or leading a discussion) and strategy , flexibility , instructional decision - making , alternative use of specific curriculum , instructional materials and classroom management .

Definitions

" A scaled down teaching encounter in class size and class time . The number of students is from 10. and the duration of period ranges from 5-20 minutes " -Allen , 1966 "

A device which provides the novice and experienced teacher alike new opportunities to improve teaching , it is a real teaching scaled down in time and size of the class , 1-5 students for 5-20 minutes

- David B Young

A teacher training procedure which reduces the teaching situation to simpler and more controlled encounter achieved by limiting the practice teaching to a specific skill and reducing teaching time and class - size .

Microteaching is a scaled down sample of teaching . The complex act of teaching is broken down onto simple components . Only one particular skill is attempted and developed during Microteaching session . The teaching act is scaled down in terms of the content of the lesson , duration of the lesson and size of the class . A student teacher teaches a short lesson of 5 to 8 minutes to a small group of learners (5 to 8) .

The lesson is self - contains and a single concept is taken up in the lesson . At the end of the lesson , the learners in the class leave and teacher trainee discusses with the supervisor . Then the teacher - trainee is given time to think about the discussion and modify his lesson and plan accordingly . The process can be repeated till desirable skill is developed . the success depends on the teach -

reteach cycle , which can be completed in about 30 minutes .

Meaning

The short lesson is recorded on an audio or video tape recorder and the trainee gets to hear and see himself immediately after the lesson . The learners who attend the lesson are asked to fill in rating questionnaires evaluating specific aspects of the lesson.

Benefits of micro-teaching

• Visual feedback (through watching a recorded lesson) has been found to provide one of the most effective means of evaluating teaching strengths and identifying areas of improvement.

• Micro-teaching enables both intrinsic (self-assessment) and extrinsic (peer-review) assessment of teaching behaviours.

• Through micro-teaching, one can seek to identify and improve these observable teaching skills and behaviours. Some such skills and observable teaching behaviours include:

• Oral presentation skills (voice modulation and articulation, enthusiasm, gestures, nonverbal cues, clarity of explanations and examples)

• Organization skills (structure of lessons, strong opening and closing, good transitions between sections, clear learning objectives, effective use of time and good pacing)

• Relating to the student (speaker engages audience, material is audience-appropriate, effective questioning and use of real-life examples)

• Effective use of teaching aids (handouts, blackboard, presentation software, overhead transparencies, props and charts, etc.).

• Aside from helping to identify teaching skills to be improved as well as teaching strengths,

micro-teaching sessions can also provide an opportunity for the following:

• Practising a part of a lecture or running an activity or explaining a procedure before you have to deliver a course or demonstrate a lab for the first time.

• Practising a guest lecture you have been asked to deliver in someone else's course.

• Practising a job talk before you visit a campus when applying for jobs.

• Practising public speaking skills before you address students for the first time.

• Polishing your questioning techniques or your opening and closing skills, if you are already an experienced instructor. \

Steps of micro-teaching It is also known as the micro-teaching cycle and includes the following six steps

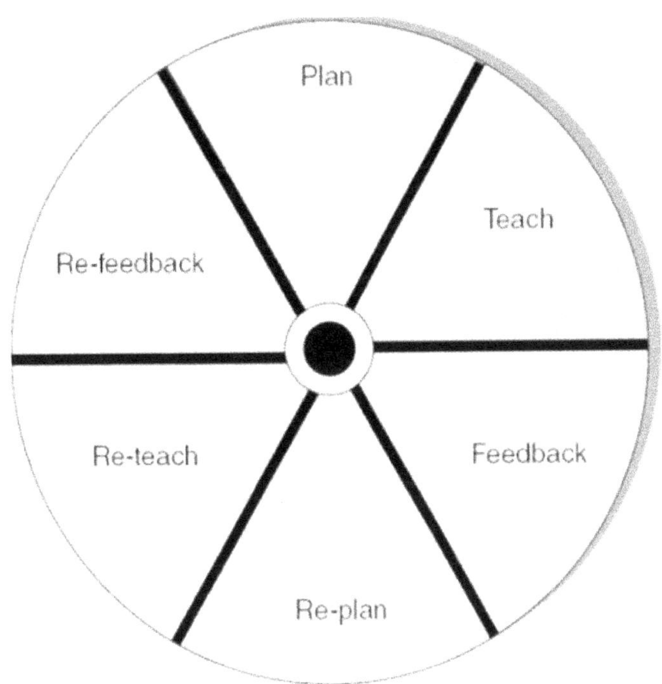

Micro-teaching cycle.

A. Plan

• This involves the selection of the topic and related content of a nature in which the use of components of the skill under practice may be made easily and conveniently.

• The topic is analyzed into different activities of the teacher and the students.

• The activities are planned in a logical sequence such that the maximum application of the components of a skill is possible.

B. Teach

• This involves the attempts of the teacher trainee to use the components of the skill in suitable situations in the process of teaching–learning per his or her planning of activities.

• If the situation is different and not as visualized in the planning of the activities, the teacher should modify his or her behaviour per the demand of the situation in the class.

• The teacher should have the courage and confidence to handle the situations arising in the class effectively.

C. Feedback

• This term refers to giving information to the teacher trainee about his performance.

• The information includes the points of strength as well as weakness relating to his or her performance.

• This helps the teacher trainee improve his or her performance in the desired direction.

D. Re-plan

The teacher trainee re-plans his lesson incorporating the points of strength and removing the points not skilfully handled during teaching in the previous attempt either on the same topic or on another topic suiting the teacher trainee for improvement.

E. Re-teach

• This involves teaching the same group of students if the topic is changed or a different group of students if the topic is the same.

• This is done to remove boredom or monotony in the students.

• The teacher trainee teaches the class with renewed courage and confidence to perform better than the previous attempt.

F. Re-feedback

This is the most important component of micro-teaching for behaviour modification of the teacher trainee in the desired direction in each and every skill practice.

Q 7. Write a short note on GROUP DISCUSSION .

= **GROUP DISCUSSION:**

Introduction:

The term group discussion stand for the discussion held within the group, i.e. interchange of ideas between students and the teacher or among a group of students.

Organizational procedure: Teacher is the leader of this group on account of his status, functions and responsibilities, usually three stages and steps are there in group discussion:

1) Planning and setting

2) Active, democratic and useful

3) Evaluating the outcome

General instruction:

1) Speak clearly, concise and not repeat yourself.

2) Speak audibly, if you don not understand, ask them to clarify in a polite manner.

3) Have to speak in a proper tone, not be harsh.

4) If you do not speak in an intelligent manner, other member assume that you are unintelligent.

5) If a statement has to be disagreed, do it in a manner that is tactful. 6) Avoid using technical terms that are not understood by the group. 7) Cultural background of individual will also play a role, how they speak.

Advantages:

1) Active participation of students.

2) Motivates students for group activities & cooperative task.

3) Motivates to listen but at the same time you can speak like a leader.

4) Student develop critical thinking, analyzing, synthesizing, evaluating, inferring, problem solving etc.

5) It teaches student not to accept any idea blindly.

Disadvantage:

1) Group discussion may go out of track.

2) Require more space than lecture.

3) It is time consuming.

4) It is difficult to monitor the progress of many small group.

5) When dominant members are not controlled it can affect the other member participation.

Q 8. Write a short note on Seminar

= **MEANING:**

1. A meeting for discussion or training.
2. Group of student meeting together to discuss topic with teacher.
3. Group of supervised students doing research or advanced study.

DEFINITION:

Seminar is a group of members come together to exchange views of current problems of to share with others their own experiences, experiments, discoveries etc.

OBJECTIVES:

1. Opportunity to participate in methods of scientific analysis and research procedure
2. To promote deeper understanding.
3. Help students to develop skills in reading and comprehension.
4. It enable students to gain experience in self evaluation and evaluation of others.

STEPS INVOLVED IN PRESENTATION OF SEMINAR:

I. Participants preparation
II. Preparation of contents
III. Preparation of environment for presentation

IV. Presentation of seminar
V. Evaluation and grading of seminar

SEMINAR FORMAT:

For discussing about disease condition contents are:

1. Introduction
2. Definition
3. Related anatomy & physiology
4. Etiology & risk factors
5. Incidence & occurrence
6. Pathophysiology
7. Diagnostic evaluation
8. Clinical manifestation
9. Management
10. Complications
11. Summary
12. Bibliography

CRITERIA FOR GOOD SEMINAR:

1. Seminar group preferably is limited to 10 to 15 students with a maximum of 25.
2. Duration of meeting is usually 1 to 2 hours.
3. Leader of discussion is the teacher.
4. Student also function as chairman.
5. Effective use of seminar method requires a background of knowledge.
6. Members must come prepared with material for presentation and discussion.

ADVANTAGES:

1. Seminar helps students to increase responsibilities.
2. It helps to do thorough study on subject.
3. It helps to improve leadership qualities.
4. It is an effective method of problem solving.
5. It will help to improve curriculum.

DISADVANTAGES:

1. It is useful only for upper division students.

2. It needs preliminary planning.

3. Members must come prepared with material for presentation and discussion.

4. Proper planning is needed to arrange seminar.

ROLE OF MEMBERS IN SEMINAR:

1) Student: • Expected to do library work • Collect the relevant content • Content should be clear and well stated • Utilize the AV Aids • Should be well prepared before presentation 2) Teacher: • Help student to select appropriate topic • Guide student to select the content • Suggest available sources of information

Q 9 . Write a short note on Field Trip .

= **INTRODUCTION:**

Direct experience with reality provides an excellent opportunity for sensory learning, field trip is a first audio- visual aid to be introduced in audio- visual media for effective learning. The specific advantage of field trip is that after the trip students just say, I have seen, instead of I have read about or I have been told.

DEFINITIONS:

Field trip is defined as an educational procedure by which the student studies first hand objectives and materials in the natural environment. -(Heidgerken) Field trip is defined as most concrete and the real best visual techniques which bring the pupil into direct contact with the real life situation. -(Bhatia)

OBJECTIVES:

To apply theory into practice

To evaluate the result of new practice

To enrich the classroom instruction

To develop observational skills

To improve social interaction among the students

To refresh students knowledge

To obtain baseline data

To develop creativity skill among students

PURPOSE:

1. It helps to furnish first hand information

2. It helps to co-relate and blend school life without side world by providing a direct touch with community situation

3. It helps to develop keenness and observational skills

4. Field trip provide opportunity to apply what is taught and verify what is learned

5. Field trip provides actual source material for study

6. Field trip helps to develop aesthetic sense in students

TYPES OF FIELD TRIPS:

1. Local school trip
2. Community trip
3. Tour or journey
4. Imaginary tour
5. Inter school visits or inter college visit
6. Individual trip

RESPONSIBILITIES OF TEACHER:

1. Check the presence of all students and see that no student is missing
2. Adequate information should be given to the students
3. Guide and supervise the students during the trip
4. Safety rules to be followed strictly throughout the trip
5. Teacher should encourage unity, discipline among the group
6. First aid box should be taken and kept in the vehicle for the trip

RESPONSIBILITIES OF STUDENT:

1. Each student is personally responsible to know place of visit, vehicle used for trip, time and place of getting on and off the vehicle
2. Student should be punctual and obey the command or instruction of the teacher
3. Student should wear suitable dress based on place of visit
4. Questions should be framed and kept ready
5. All luggage of the student should be labeled and should be ready on time for departure
6. Each student should take notes whenever they are instructed to take

ADVANTAGES:

1. Observation of active participation with reality
2. Opportunity for co-operative group work and sharing responsibilities
3. Enable the students to develop self confidence
4. Ensure close contacts with reality
5. It increases the variability
6. It is good method for individual motivation
7. **It gives relief from monotonous life of classroom**

DISADVANTAGE:

1. Costly in time and transport
2. Field trip possible for limited audience only
3. Requires careful planning for its effectiveness
4. Distracters cannot be controlled
5. Advance knowledge regarding the place should be known to teachers
6. Finding appropriate site may be difficult
7. Schedules are difficult to maintain .

Q 11 . Write a short note on Classroom management

= Classroom management

The principal is the head of an institution and a class teacher is the head of a class. Institutional management comes under the preview of the head of the institution but classroom management is the ultimate responsibility of the class teacher.

The class teacher is expected to manage his class. Academic success of an institution principally depends on efficient class management by a competent class teacher. A teacher must possess some core qualities for efficient management of a class such as general academic proficiency, professional and managerial efficiency and positive personality traits.

Definitions of classroom management

Classroom management is an organizational function in which tasks are performed in a variety of settings, resulting in the inculcation of certain values such as human respect, personal integrity, self-direction and group cohesion etc. —Johanson and Brooks

Classroom management is a system of action and activities are managed in classroom to induce learning through teacher–taught relationship.

Teacher and students are the basic components for managing classroom activities. (Operational meaning)

Dimensions of classroom management

In behavioural terms, classroom management can be classified in four different dimensions:

1. **physical or environmental dimension,**
2. **psychological dimension,**
3. **ethical dimension, and social and**
4. **cultural dimension of classroom management .**

Physical/environmental dimension: Physical or environmental dimension of classroom management includes light and ventilation of the classroom, seating arrangement for students, availability and functioning of blackboard and/or other audiovisual facilities in classroom, offering aesthetic academic environment inside and/ or outside classroom. A teacher as a classroom manager should ensure the optimum and efficient management of these physical or environment facilities/services which are essential for overall learning in the students.

Psychological dimension: Psychological dimension of classroom management is considered similar to software of the computer; without its presence mere hardware (physical/ environmental dimension) is of no use and vice versa. Psychological classroom management includes infusion of motivation in students to promote the learning process. Motivation could be infused verbally or nonverbally through continuous feedback, behavioural reinforcement and positive encouragement in students. Psychological dimension of classroom management plays a pivotal role in the overall management of a classroom.

Social and cultural dimension: A classroom is a miniature replica of an institution as well as of the society. The new society is shaped in the classroom through its desirable social and cultural environment. Classroom management involves the relationship of social and cultural environment in its overall management which depends on certain factors such as the teacher–taught relationship, relationship among students, relationship among teachers, relationship between teachers and the head of the institution. A teacher must know the background of his students and their entering behaviour, learning activities and interests.

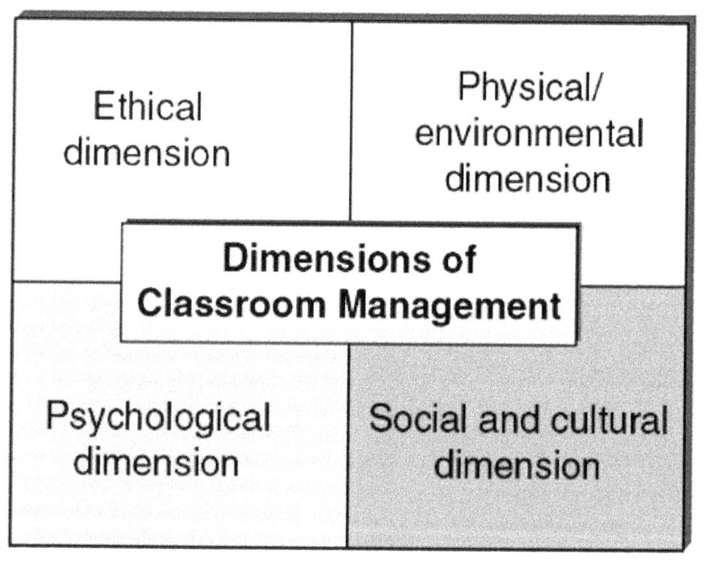

Dimensions of classroom management.

Ethical dimension: The ethical dimension of classroom management is concerned with feelings, attitudes, values and ethical aspects of students. A teacher is the manager of the class and an ideal to his students. He should look like and behave like a teacher. Further, the teacher should maintain classroom code and conduct which should be value based or ethics oriented.

Specific principles of classroom management

Specific principles of classroom management can be adapted and used in certain specific situations and can be very helpful for overall classroom management. These are discussed below:

- **Planning**: Plan independent activities as well as organized lessons so students can be motivated to achieve their educational goals.
- **Encouragement**: Encourage effort and cues and reinforce positive and appropriate behaviour so students can be motivated for learning.
- **Responsibility**: Let students assume independent responsibility so they can develop a sense of responsibility and accountability towards their own education.
- **Minimum disruption:** Teachers must ensure that there is minimal disruption in natural learning among the students so they can have uninterrupted natural learning.
- **Clear rules:** The rules established for the students must be crystal clear so that ambiguity can be avoided and following rules and their implementation becomes easy.
- **Reward and punishment**: Students must be rewarded for their behaviour so they can be reinforced for repeating positive behaviour and discouraged from negative behaviour.
- **Conducive learning environment:** It is believed that the environment influences a person more than anything else. Therefore, a conducive teaching–learning environment can help a classteacher achieve the expected positive behaviour in students.

Classroom management problems

- **Inadequate light and ventilation**: Effective classroom work can take place only in a congenial classroom atmosphere that includes adequate light and ventilation, temperature, furniture, seats, etc. Inadequate light and ventilation can create problems for the student. It has an adverse effect on their learning as well as health.

- **Inadequate furniture and lack of conducive seating environment**: In the absence of proper seating arrangements, the students find themselves uneasy and uncomfortable. They do not feel like working wholeheartedly. They find it difficult to concentrate on learning in the class.
- **Overcrowded classrooms**: It is not possible for the teacher to teach effectively in a fully packed classroom. The teacher cannot give individual attention to all students. Therefore, the number of students in a class should not exceed more than 50.
- **Inadequate apparatus:** In an overcrowded class, it is difficult to provide adequate equipment to all students affecting their learning.
- Lack of routine: Breaking a routine creates confusion, chaos, disorder and indiscipline in the class. Routine should be followed in taking roll-calls, performing practicals, entering or leaving the classroom and other activities.
- **Lack of adequate distance between classrooms**: Many classrooms are so near each other that the noise of one class disturbs students sitting in other classrooms. This can affect their studies.
- **Problems of indiscipline:** Absenteeism among teachers and the taught can also affect classroom teaching.
- **Poor teacher–taught interpersonal relationship**: In ancient times, there was a strong teacher–pupil relationship; however with the present changing cultural values, there is a lack of teacher–taught relationship these days that ultimately affects the teaching–learning outcome in an institution.

Q 13 .Role of a teacher in classroom management .

= ***Role of a teacher in classroom management***

A teacher plays a pivotal role in classroom management because he is the central component of classroom management and has the authority, responsibility and accountability to manage a class. He plays variety of roles such as teacher, manager, philosopher, guide, researcher and leader. Efficient classroom management demands strong interpersonal relationship skills in a teacher, where he/she needs to build strong interpersonal relationship with students, colleagues, head of the institution and even parents of students and society as a whole. The main roles of the teacher in classroom management are as follows .

- **Teacher:** The core aim of classroom management is to achieve the expected outcome of the particular teaching–learning process. Therefore, the primary role of the teacher in classroom management is functioning efficiently as a teacher.
- **Manager:** Classroom management demands managerial skills from teachers. They are expected to perform responsibilities of planning, organizing, supervising, directing, coordinating and controlling the teaching–learning process.
- **Leader:** The teacher is expected to lead the class as a classroom manager for its overall functioning and taking desired messages to higher authorities and convincing them with the expected demands.

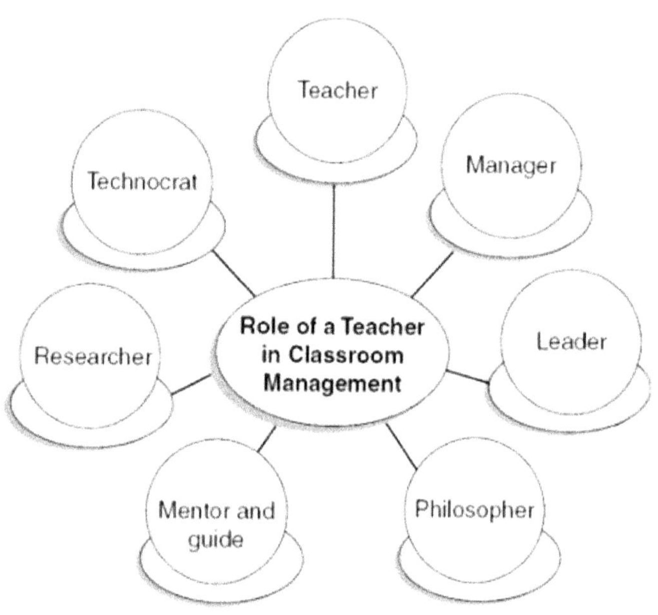

Role of the teacher in classroom management.

- **Philosopher:** The teacher is expected to have a strong hold and mastery over the subject content that has to be delivered to students. In addition, a teacher is expected to teach moral values, ethics and discipline to the students.
- **Mentor and guide**: Each of us requires a mentor or guide to help us choose the right path in life. Students also require a mentor or guide to help them take the right decisions for learning activities. Therefore, a teacher is expected to perform the role of a mentor or guide for a particular group of students to solve their personal as well teaching–learning related problems.

• **Researcher:** Solutions for problems are generated through research. A teacher also faces a lot of problems related to classroom management that can be easily solved by generating evidence-based solutions generated through action research. Therefore, a teacher must act as researcher to generate the empirical solutions for classroom management related problems.

• **Technocrat:** Advancement in science and technology has offered a wide range of technologically sophisticated audiovisual aids to the educational institutions. A teacher must be technologically skilled to operate and manage these technologically sophisticated audiovisual aids as and when required.

Q 13 . Programmed instructions

= Programmed instructions .

The instructions provided by a teaching machine or programmed textbook are referred to as programmed instructions.

• According to J.E. Espich and Bill Williams, 'programmed instruction is a planned sequence of experiences, leading to proficiency, in terms of stimulus–response relationship that have proven to be effective'.

• According to Susan Markle (1969), 'programmed instruction is a method of designing reproducible sequence of instructional events to produce a measurable consistent effect on a behaviour of each and every acceptable student'.

I. Characteristics of programmed instructions

• The subject matter is broken down into small steps called frames and arranged sequentially.

• Frequent response of the student is required.

• There is an immediate confirmation of the right answer or correction of wrong answers given by the learners, i.e. 'self-correcting feature'.

• The content and sequence of the frames are subjected to actual try out by students and are revised on the basis of data gathered by the programmer, i.e. 'diagnostic feature'.

- Each student progresses at his own pace without any threat of being exposed to any humiliation in a heterogeneous class.
- The assumption about the learner is clearly stated in the programmed learning materials.
- The objectives underlying programming instructions are defined explicitly and in operational terms so that the terminal behaviour is made observable and measurable.
- The interaction between the learner and the programme is emphasized in programmed learning.
- In a programmed material, continuous evaluation is possible by recording the student's response.
- The strategy provides sufficient situations for teaching the students to discriminate between a range of possibilities and reduce generalizations.

Advantages of programmed instructions

- Programmed instructions are more successful in critical sagacity (discernment) of the logic of various subjects and inspiring students' creative thinking and judgement.
- Good teachers are freed from the humdrum of routine classroom activity and they are in a position to devote their time to more creative activities.
- Some educationists fear that the programmed instructions will deteriorate the quality of instruction. On the other hand, their use has improved the quality of education in general.
- The use of programmed instructions has brought a revolution in the social setting of the classroom. Many emotional and social problems have been eliminated and problems of discipline have been solved automatically.
- Programmed instruction is a great thrust in the direction of individualized instruction. A well-organized programmed instructional device is tailored to cater to the needs of individual students of the class.
- It helps the teacher diagnose the problems of the individual learner.

• By presenting the material in small segments of information, i.e. frames, it makes learning an interesting game in which the learner is challenged by his own capabilities.

Disadvantages of programmed instructions

• Programmed instruction does not eliminate competition or grades as often claimed.

• Mere manipulation of machine is not rewarding to children as Skinner seems to think. Once the novelty wears and if, at the start, too many errors appear, the students lose interest and motivation. Later reinforcements often do not accelerate learning.

• Programmed instructions restrict the learner's freedom of choice resulting in cramping of his imagination and initiative.

• Operant conditioning is found successful only with some students in some cases and not in all. Programmed instructions ignore or make inadequate provisions for variables like cognitive, personality and motivational variables.

• The teacher–pupil contact, which is so vital for development of human personality and relationship, is completely lost.

• In language learning, speech is equally important as development of reading and comprehension skills. There is no scope for providing this experience.

Q 14 . Computer-assisted learning Application of computers in nursing

= Computer-assisted learning

The word computer is derived from the word compute, which means to calculate justifying its usefulness.

A computer is an electronic machine, which works under the control of a stored programme, automatically acccpting processing of data to producing designed results. Computer-assisted learning (CAL) is also known as computer-assisted instruction (CAI).

Application of computers in nursing

The main areas for the application of computers in nursing are as follows.

I. Education

• Knowledge of computers can be applied to prepare slides in MS PowerPoint on the topics to be taught to students.

• Knowledge of multimedia helps the nursing teachers and students teach effectively

. • Education through internet and CAL has simplified education in nursing schools.

• A computer aids in learning and instructions:

• By providing information and instructions.

• By asking questions.

• By doing difficult calculations.

• By being tireless and repetitive.

• By simulated process.

• By selecting the right speed for providing information to individual learners.

II. Administration

• Preparing records of nursing students by lecturers and nursing superintendent.

• Preparing and maintaining records of assessment and results.

• Preparing duty rosters that saves time.

• Preparing drafts of a plan annually, monthly and weekly.

III. Hospital

• Computers keep records of patient's health status during hospital stay and OPD.

• Hospital information management system (HIMS) helps to have access to the patient treatment chart, operation list or anaesthetic record; this is possible with computer knowledge.

• Computer helps nurses manage routine documents in a fraction of a time, which may otherwise take up a lot of time manually.

• It increases productivity of nurses.

• Other functions in hospitals, i.e. automatic generation of reminder letters, determination of milestones, are performed with the help of appropriate softwares.

Features of HIMS

• Data is retrieved quickly and easily.

• Entry of data is easy.

• It has a high degree of security of data.

• Data validation is stringent. Benefits of HIMS

• Improvement in the doctor's productivity.

• Reduced patient waiting time.

• Eliminating wastage of stationary.

• Prompt medical attention.

• Accuracy and timeliness of data.

• Eliminating any possibility of mixing of blood samples

. • Authorization check and accuracy of billing.

• Prompt issue of medication for patients.

• Maintaining inventory of medication.

• Safe recording of data and saving the time that has to be spent in the medical record department.

• Carrying legal value.

• Prescribing diet from the ward through a computer.

• Giving secret code to prevent manipulation for security reasons.

• Blood bank module for donor registration and certification helps make referrals within the hospital, prepare duty rosters, OT scheduling, diagnostic appointments and patient records.

IV. Research work

• Computers are used to get information on the research works being carried out via the internet.

• They help support research findings with other research that has been carried out.

• Knowledge of computers helps nurses increase their productivity and provide the best patient centred care.

A knowledge of computers reduces the time taken to for documentation which usually takes time when done manually.

Q 15 . Clinical teaching methods

= **Clinical teaching methods**

Nurses need learning in three domains i.e. cognitive, affective and psychomotor. However, psychomotor domain of learning is most essential in nursing discipline because nurses need to have hands-on skills to provide best quality nursing care to their patients or clients.

Therefore, it is essential for nurse educators to provide clinical teaching through most robust and advanced methods, so that nursing students can swiftly learn the real-life clinical knowledge and clinical skills.

According to Schweer (1972), 'clinical teaching is a vehicle that provides students with the opportunity to translate basic theoretical knowledge into the learning of a variety of intellectual and psychomotor skills needed to provide patient centred quality nursing care'.

I. Responsibilities of clinical teacher

1. Plan and implement the clinical learning experiences through most effective methods of clinical teaching.
2. Plan and prepare required clinical area and needed resources for effective clinical experiences.
3. Orient the new group of students to the clinical environment to promote their adaptation to the new clinical setting.
4. Facilitate in arranging all the essential resources required for the clinical learning.
5. Demonstrating clinical nursing skills and motivating the students to carryout return demonstrations to ensure that they have acquired the required clinical learning.
6. Helping the students to gradually become independent in performing the learned clinical knowledge and skills.
7. Assessing the students to ensure that they have achieved optimum level of desired learning in the particular clinical field/ area.
8. Keep himself/herself updated with most advanced and effective methods of clinical teaching.

II. Qualities of a good clinical teacher

1. Available, approachable and nonthreatening.

2. Resourceful.
3. Clinically competent.
4. Nonjudgmental.
5. Enthusiastic and passionate in clinical teaching and learning.
6. Empathetic and tolerant.
7. Three 'A' for qualities of clinical teacher are – Ability (attitude, knowledge and clinical skills). – Availability (physical presence of teacher in clinical setting/bedside). – Affability (approachable, affectionate, gentle, gracious and friendly).

Type of Clinical Teaching Method

1. Nursing case study :

Nursing case study is in-depth study and analysis of progress of a patient with specific disease, who received nursing care for an extended period ranging between 7 and 10 days. In the case study, students get an opportunity to understand the effects of particular nursing interventions on specific nursing problems/diagnoses.

2. Nursing case presentation

Nursing case presentation refers to a formal discussion of a particular patient in details regarding medical diagnosis, clinical features, diagnostic tests, medical/surgical treatment, nursing assessment findings, identified nursing problems and best possible planned nursing care interventions considering best recommended practices.

3. Nursing rounds

It is a clinical teaching method in which a group of nursing students are taken for a selected patient's bedside visit by one or more nursing faculties to discuss about the progress of the patient and further plan of care, which provides the students first-hand clinical learning experiences.

4. Bedside nursing clinics

Bedside nursing clinic is a method of clinical teaching, which is also called as bedside teaching where a small group of students are taught about a disease condition or nursing care practices directly on a real patient at bedside, which provides rich opportunity of visual, auditory, tactile and olfactory experiences.

5. Nursing assignments

Nursing assignment refers to the assignment of particular patient or nursing task of the patient to the nursing students under the direct supervision of nursing teacher, where he/she gets an opportunity to obtain direct clinical learning experiences.

6. Nursing care conferences

Conference is the act of coming together of two or more nursing individuals in a formal meeting for the purpose of giving or exchanging ideas or in a formal discussion of problems and their possible solutions. It could be a group or individual activity based on the needs and purposes of conference.

7. Health team conference

Health team conference is a multidisciplinary team activity, where professionals from different discipline formally meet together to discuss particular case or issue of the common interest.

8. Process recording

Process recording is a method of clinical teaching in which students get an opportunity to directly interact with patient in the supervision of clinical faculty where he/she gets a chance to obtain skills of communication, history taking, critical thinking and recording of interaction.

9. Field visits

Field visit is defined as a planned activity to take the students out of classroom for an observation of particular place, persons, organization or situation

Q 16. Explain in detail Project method of teaching .

= The project method has been recognized as a teaching technique since many years; it has its primary inception in the field of agriculture sciences where students carried out some planned creative activities in a natural environment or a planned work field to produce certain products. Later it was used in vocational education programmes. The essential characteristics of the project method are planned activity of the individual and production of tangible results. This method is a teaching method where students learn to work individually or in a group to achieve preplanned learning objectives.

Characteristics of a good project method

• The method aims at teaching the learner to get the best out of life.

• An attempt to use experience, trust and the best master whose lessons are unforgettable.

• The project method gives an opportunity for self-expression.

• The experiments of the project method want to reset the whole curriculum and break all barriers of the subject matter.

• The project matter proposes the whole sequence of activities involved in complete understanding.

• A project can be a large unit of appreciational learning or of attitude development that increases motor skills and technical knowledge.

• A project is a play activity and learners are engaged in carrying out the activity.

• The project method is a complete surrender to the learner's point of view.

• In the project method the procedure of the school is liable to be determined by the technique of a workshop because the individual learns much better from his own activity than by constant instruction. • An attempt is made to establish a positive relation with life.

• The project method lends itself naturally to group work.

• It is a large unit plan of teaching.

• The method seeks to have individuals see and understand life in its unity.

The role of teacher in the project method

• The teacher has to skilfully guide in the selection.

• The student has to be given help when required.

• The teacher should be good prompter.

• The relations of the teacher and students should be much closer and informal than in ordinary classroom teaching.

• The teacher is like a friend with rich and mature experience.

• The teacher acts as a director, i.e. the teacher's psychological knowledge must be thorough and specific.

• The teacher must be a keen observer and a true sympathizer.

• The teacher should be a store house of information and knowledge.

Advantages of the project method

• It follows the psychological laws of learning:

• Law of readiness. • Law of exercise. • Law of effect.

• It gives freedom to the students.

• It suited to the psychological concept of maturation.

• It drives social values.

• It trains for social adjustments.

• It saves children from insincerity and superficiality.

• It trains for a democratic way of life.

• It promotes learning through practical problem saving.

• It helps the students and teachers grow. The student stimulated by and encouraged in his exploration of many materials will ultimately approach other areas of learning in a similar manner. The teacher will grow in his or her understanding of a child's creative developments.

• It confers on school work a much needed sense of reality.

• It sets up an intrinsic standard of evaluation.

• It leads to satisfaction of completing the whole task.

• It is economical; the students take more interest and learn in the shortest possible time.

• It is ideal for science work, handicrafts and practical geography and dramatic work literature.

Disadvantages of the project method

• The role of communication is subordinated to the glorification of active learning.

• The practical difficulties of covering a syllabus rule out the project method as the basis of teaching in most schools.

• It is time-consuming and limited by availability and cost of materials.

- It is most valuable in students with lesser academic interest, for it provides an opportunity for the practical enthusiast.
- It leaves gaps in student knowledge.
- It may be too ambitious: beyond a student's capacity.
- Opportunity for the correlation with the academic subjects is extremely limited.
- In this method instructions are more planned; therefore it may disturb the regular instructional schedule.
- It involves difficulty to ensure any kind of systematic progress in instructions.
- A complete reorganization of the school is needed for a new teacher.
- Children may ignore maxims, working from simple to complex.
- Time-bound projects are introduced artificially and may require more than necessary help.
- Projects may be adopted or abandoned at will.
- The project approach often results in an incomplete mastery of the tools of learning, which are essential to student education later.

Q 17 . Define lesson plan.

= Lesson planning Lesson planning is an important activity of daily teaching. The lesson plan might include the main points to be covered in the lesson activities for the students to do, questions related to the topic being taught and some form of assessment for the realization of stipulated instructional objectives. It indicates clearly what has already been done, what the students are to do, how the students are to be engaged in various activities and what activities are to be pursued. Lesson planning is the heart of effective teaching.

Definitions of lesson plan

Lesson plan is the title given to a statement of achievement to be realized and specific meanings by which these are to be attained as a result of the activities engaged during the period. —N.L. Bossing

Daily lesson planning involves defining the objectives, selecting and arranging the subject matter and determining the method of procedure.

Q 19 Write the purposes of lesson plan.

= Significance and importance of a lesson plan

- In a teaching education programme, the lesson plan provides guidelines to students and the teacher during their teaching–learning practices.
- It helps in achieving the definite objectives.
- It makes teaching systematic, orderly and economical.
- It helps teachers overcome feelings of nervousness and insecurity and gives them confidence to face the class.
- It links new knowledge with previous knowledge acquired by a student. • It prepares pivotal questions and illustrations.
- It enables the teacher evaluate his work as the lesson proceeds.
- It helps the teacher use a wider variety of teaching materials and learning activities in the classroom through a wider acquaintance with resources.
- It also helps the teacher plan the teaching–learning process per the availability and accessibility of resource materials.

Q 20 .Prepare the lesson plan on the topic

= Format of a lesson plan An effective lesson must have the following format

I. **Cover page:** This page must include topic of lesson, date of submission, name of supervisor, and name and details of the presenting teacher.

II. **First page:** This page must include the following basic information: Basic lesson plan information:

• Subject	: Communication and Education Technology
• Name of topic	: Assessment of learning needs
• Name of student's teacher	: Ms Jasveen Kaur
• Name of supervisor	: Dr Suresh K. Sharma
• Date of teaching	: ____________
• Time of teaching	: ____________
• Venue of teaching	: Lecturer Theater No. 3
• Group	: B.Sc. (N) 2nd year students
• Size of group	: 25
• Method of teaching	: Lecture cum discussion
• Duration	: ___ minutes
• AV Aids	: PowerPoint Presentation

Previous knowledge: The group has some knowledge about the topic: Assessment of learning needs.

General objective: At the end of the class, students will be able to acquire knowledge about assessment of learning needs.

Specific objectives: At the end of teaching, students will be able to

- Define various terms related to assessment of learning needs.
- Explain about historical perspective.
- Enlist types of assessment.
- Enumerate principles of assessment for learning.
- Describe purposes of conducting assessment of learning needs.

III. Main body of lesson plan:

S. No.	Time	Contributory Objective	Content Matter	Teaching–Learning Activities	
				AV Aids	*Evaluation*

Appendix of lesson plan: This includes giving the assignment to students and recommending further reading, writing the bibliography and references.

Q 21 Steps of lesson planning .

= Steps of lesson planning

1. Preparation or introduction: Exploration of the student's knowledge helps to lead them on to the lesson. The teacher needs to prepare the students to receive new knowledge.

2. Presentation: The aim of the lesson should be clearly stated before presentation of the subject matter, which helps both the teacher and students have common pursuit.

3. Comparison or association: Quote examples and associate facts with two examples so that learners can understand easily and arrive at generalizations on their own.

4. Generalizations: The knowledge presented by the teacher should be thought-provoking, innovating and stimulating to assist the students generalize the situation.

5. Application: The students should be able to make use of the knowledge acquired and test the validity of the generalization arrived at in theory. It has to apply in the clinical field to make learning more permanent and worthwhile.

6. Recapitulation: The teacher has to ask suitable, stimulating and pivotal questions on the topic. The answer will give feedback to the teacher regarding the efficacy of the method of teaching and he can decide whether or not clarification is needed.

Q 22 . Essential characteristics of a good lesson plan

=The essential characteristics of a lesson are discussed below

- **Clearly written:** Lesson plans must preferably be in written form. It must be appropriately written and depict who will be taught, who will teach, when will be taught, where the class will be taken, what will be taught, why it will be taught, how it will be taught and what should be expected from students after the lesson.
- **Definite aim and objectives:** A good lesson plan must have clearly defined aim and objectives that very clearly specify the purpose of the lesson and the purpose of each activity included in the lesson plan.
- **Extension of existing knowledge: The** topic of a lesson plan should be planned in a consecutive sequence of the previously taught topics or existing knowledge for better understanding of the topic. It should not be a repetition nor an isolated topic plan.
- **Simple and comprehensive:** Each lesson plan must be simple, lucid, concise and precise and must include all activities that are expected to be carried out by a teacher in classroom during the teaching–learning process comprehensively.
- **Flexible plan:** A planned lesson must not be rigid; it must be flexible to adopt the changes expected to arise in specific classroom situations. A flexible lesson plan facilities the teacher adapt to specific incidental situations in the classroom.
- **Ensure active teaching–learning process:** A good lesson plan ensures active participation of both the teacher and the student for effective achievement of educational objectives. A passive lesson plan fails to motivate the teacher and/or the student for an effective teaching–learning activity outcome.
- **Division with essence of wholesomeness:** A lesson plan must be divided into subsections for better presentation; however, its wholesomeness must not be distorted. A logical sequence and efficient cohesion of the subsections of the lesson may help in the preservation of the lesson plan's wholesomeness.

- **Individualized and customized:** The content of the lesson plan should be designed according to the needs, interests, abilities and level of the students. This individualized and customized approach helps the teacher achieve the expected aim of a lesson plan.
- **Feasibility and significance:** A lesson plan must be planned in a manner that it is feasible in terms of time and available resources. It must be as practical as possible without overestimations in a hypothetical manner. In addition, a lesson plan must have significance to a particular group of students because nonsignificant topics fail to create interest in learners as well as the teacher. Therefore, the teaching–learning activity may not be fruitful without the significance of a lesson/topic.
- **Proceed from general to specific:** A lesson plan must be planned such that it proceeds from general or basic knowledge to specific knowledge so students can easily understand the lesson.
- **Completeness:** A good lesson plan must be complete in itself without leaving any essential component like topic of the lesson, general and specific objectives, content, teacher–student activity and methods of presentation, audiovisual aids, question to be asked for students, summary, recapitalized and assignment for the students.
- Inclusion of summary, recapitalization, bibliography and student assignment: In addition to a basic introductory plan and body of the lesson, the lesson plan must include the summary, recapitalization, bibliography and student assignment.

CHAPTER SEVEN

EDUCATIONAL MEDIA

SHORT ANSWER QUESTIONS

Q 1 . Principles of Audio Visual Aids.

= **Definition**

Audio-visual aids are those sensory objects or images which initiates or stimulate and reinforce learning. —Burton

Audio-visual aids are those aids which help in completing the triangular process of learning i.e. motivation, classification and stimulation. —Carter V. Good

Principles for using audiovisual aids

The following principles must be kept in mind for the effective use of audiovisual aids.

- **Principle of selection:**

Selection of an audiovisual aid must be based on the basic characteristics of a learner, teacher, educational material, educational institution and the philosophy and objectives of the teaching–learning process. The basic characteristics of a learner that should be considered are age, class, mental ability and interest. For selecting a teaching tool, it must be ensured that teachers have the knowledge, ability and attitude to use a specific audiovisual aid. Furthermore, educational media must be selected according to the type of educational content delivered, resources and readiness of the educational institution. Moreover, educational media must be the best substitute for the real-life experience.

- **Principle of preparation:**

To promote the efficient use of audiovisual aids, sound preparation is required in special reference to infrastructure, training of teachers and money for the preparation and maintenance of audiovisual aids. Primarily, self-made, cost-effective, locally available and teacher–taught friendly audiovisual aids must be used.

- **Principle of physical control:**

For the efficient use and durability of audiovisual aids, it is necessary to have an appropriate control of the physical environment, e.g. a proper place for storage, appropriate environmental temperature, proper cleanliness. An appropriate physical control for audiovisual aids in the classroom and institution promotes the working, durability and hindrance-free use of the audiovisual aids.

- **Principle of proper presentation:**

The presentation of the teaching aid is the operation stage. The teachers must carefully ensure that the audiovisual aid is in good working condition. They should acquaint themselves with all the operating systems so that aids can be handled without any undue discomfort. Furthermore, teaching aids must be presented in a manner that every student can visualize them with the greatest comfort and it should catch the attention of students and ultimately enhance learning in the learners.

- **Principle of response:**

Teachers must ensure that students respond to the stimulus provided by the audiovisual aids so that they can judge the effectiveness of the audiovisual aid in promoting learning in students. In absence of students' response, teachers will not be able to evaluate the effectiveness of the teaching aids in the achievement of educational objectives.

- **Principle of evaluation:**

Evaluation is one of the most essential principles because it conveys the efficacy of a particular teaching aid. The teachers can modify their plans of audiovisual aids used in light of the results of evaluation of a particular audiovisual aid. Evaluation of audiovisual aids should be made a regular and continuous process so that timely action can be taken and educational objectives can be achieved without any undue inconvenience and delay.

• **Other miscellaneous principles:**

Some additional miscellaneous principles for the use of audiovisual aids are as follows:

• Audiovisual materials should be utilized as an integral part of the educational programme.

• Educational aids should be central to the teaching–learning process, under special direction and leadership in educational objectives.

• An advisory committee must be consulted in the selection and utilization of audiovisual materials for different group of students.

• Educational aids and educational materials must be mutually flexible so they can be adapted based on the needs.

• Ethical and legal aspects should be considered in the production and the utilization of educational communication media.

Q 3. Purposes of audiovisual aids

= Audio-visual aids are those sensory objects or images which initiates or stimulate and reinforce learning. —Burton

Audio-visual aids are those aids which help in completing the triangular process of learning i.e. motivation, classification and stimulation. —Carter V. Good

Purposes of audiovisual aids

Audiovisual aids enhance clarity in communication, provide diversity in the methods of teaching and increase the forcefulness of the subjects being learned or taught. Furthermore, students get direct experience of real-life situations or direct sensory experiences or symbolic experiences through the use of audiovisual aids.

Moreover, some essential purposes of the audiovisual aids are as follows:

- They help in effective perceptual and conceptual learning.
- They are helpful in capturing and sustaining the attention of students.
- They are helpful in new learning. New things are interpreted in terms of past experiences.
- Imagery helps preserve and clarify past experiences and provides near realistic experience.
- They increase and sustain attention, concentration and the personal involvement of students in actual learning.
- They create interest, secure attention and motivate students to learn.
- It is easier to understand any given concept through the use of sensory aids.
- They help in saving energy and time of both the teachers and students.
- They give the student an opportunity to touch, feel and see a model, map, picture or specimen and provide a sensory stimulus to enhance learning.
- They provide for purposeful self-activity and student participation. • They help provide concreteness, realism and lifelikeness in the teaching–learning process.
- Pictures are helpful in studying concrete reality to gain actual meaning.
- They help explicate and increase the meaningfulness of abstract concepts.
- Concrete experience helps combat the tendency to abstractness.
- Visual materials give definite meaning to words.
- They bring remote events of either space or time into the classroom.

• They serve as an open window through which the student can view the world or its entire phenomenon.

• They introduce an opportunity for situational or field type of learning as contrasted with the linear order verbal and written communication.

• It provides direct experience to the student in the clinical setting and observation experience through field trips or such other media. • They provide, facilitate and advance the process of applying what is learned to realistic performance and life situations.

• They can meet individual demands.

• They are useful for the education of masses.

Q 5 Write a types of different audiovisual aids

= A basic classification of the types of different audiovisual aids is given below.

I. Auditory aids

- Radio	- Tape and disc recordings	- Mike (public address system)
- Phonograms	- Megaphone	- Microphone
- Gramophone	- Language laboratories	- Tape recorder

II. Nonprojected/Unprojected visual aids: included both graphical and display aids

- Models	- Pictures	- Charts
- Flannel boards	- Graphs	- Chalkboards
- Cartoons and comics	- Maps	- Photographs
- Flash cards	- Illustrations	- Posters and printed media

III. Projected visual aids

- Epidiascope	- Slide projector	- Overhead projector
- Film projector	- Opaque projector	- LCD (liquid crystal display)

IV. Audiovisual aids

- Television, VCR/VCD	- Video and camera	- Sound-motion pictures

V. Activity aid

- Field trips	- Model making	- Collection of material
- Exhibition	- Demonstration	- Computer-assisted instructions
		- Programmed instructions

VI. Traditional media

- Puppets	- Dramas	- Folk songs and folk dance

Q 6. Classification of Av Aids .

=

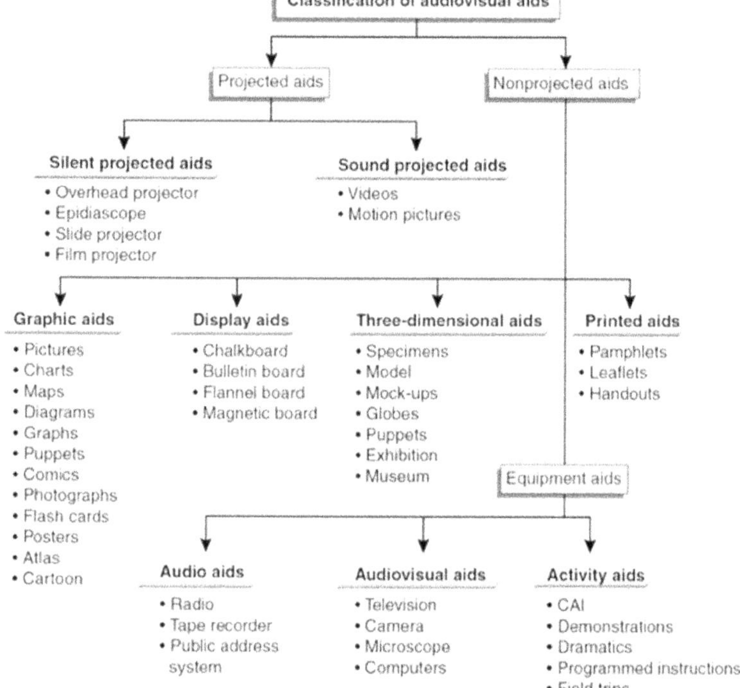

Q 7 . Write a Note on a Graphical teaching aids

= **Graphical teaching aids**

The word graphics is derived from the Greek word graphikos that means visual presentations on some surface such as a wall, canvas, computer screen, paper or stone to brand, inform, illustrate or entertain. Graphics can be functional or artistic. The latter can be a recorded version, such as a photograph, or an interpretation by a scientist to highlight the essential features, or an artist, in which case the distinction with imaginary graphics may become blurred.

There are multiple graphic aids that can be used in today's classroom and motivate students to learn. The most commonly used graphical teaching aids include chalkboard, chart, graphs, posters, flash cards, flannel board, bulletin board and cartoons, which are discussed below.

I. Chalkboard/blackboard

A blackboard is any dark-coloured, flat, smooth surface on which one can write or draw with a chalk (Fig. 8.5). It is one of the oldest and simplest visual aids. A chalkboard is also known as a blackboard that is a dark-coloured writing surface especially black or green in colour used for classroom teaching by writing or drawing illustrations using sticks of chalks. Originally, chalkboards were prepared using smooth, thin sheets of slate or stone of black or dark grey colour. However, in the new era, green coloured blackboards are becoming more popular because of their better compatibility viewers' vision.

I. Chart

A chart is a combination of pictorial, graphic and numerical materials, which presents a clear visual summary (Fig. 8.6). It is a diagnostic representation of facts and ideas. The main function of the chart is always to show relationships such as comparisons, relative amounts, developments, processes, classification and organization. Edgar Dale defines charts as, 'a visual symbol summarizing, comparing, contrasting or performing other helpful services in explaining subject-matter'.

III. Graphs

Graphs are illustrations to present numerical and statistical data using dots, lines, shapes, colours and pictures. Graphical presentation is a visual art based on the use of visual symbolic and visual-abstract forms. They depict numerical, quantitative relationship or statistical data represented in the form of visual symbols. The common types of graphs are bar graph, line graph, pictorial graphs, histograms, pie graph and cumulative frequency graph.

IV. Posters

S.L. Ahulawalia says 'a poster is a pictorial device designed to attract attention and communicate a story, a fact, an idea, or an image rapidly and clearly'. In other words, a poster is a 'placard, usually pictorial or decorative, utilizing an emotional appeal to convey a message aimed at reinforcing an attitude or urging a course of action'. Posters are generally used for conveying a specific message, teaching a particular thing, giving a general idea, etc. Posters exert great influence on the observer

The poster can be further defined as a graphic representation of some strong emotional appeal that is carried through a combination of graphic aids like pictures, cartoons lettering and other visual arts on a placard. Posters are the graphic aids with short quick and typical messages with attention capturing paintings.

IV. **Flash cards**

Flash cards are used for the presentation of an idea in the form of posters, pictures, words and sentences (Fig. 8.14). A single card or a whole series may be flashed in front of the class. In other words, flash cards are a set of pictured paper cards of varying sizes that are flashed one by one in a logical sequence. Flash cards can be self-made or commercially prepared and are made up of a chart or drawing paper or plain paper using colours or ink on them for drawings.

I. **Bulletin board**

A bulletin board is a display board that shows the visual learning material on a specific subject. It is a soft board that holds pins or tags. It is a simple device placed either indoors or outdoors. Items like photographs, publications, posters, newspaper cut-outs are generally displayed

II. **Cartoons**

A cartoon is a humorous caricature which gives a subtle message. In a cartoon, the features of objects and people are exaggerated along with their general symbols. In short, a cartoon is a figurative and subtle graphic aid. It is a metaphoric representation of reality and makes learning more interesting and effective, as it creates a strong appeal to the emotions. A cartoon is an interpretative illustration which uses symbols to portray an opinion, a scene or a situation

Q 8. Guidelines for preparing and using a poster & Advantages of a poster , Limitations of a poster

= 'a poster is a pictorial device designed to attract attention and communicate a story, a fact, an idea, or an image rapidly and clearly'. In other words, a poster is a 'placard, usually pictorial or decorative, utilizing an emotional appeal to convey a message aimed at reinforcing an attitude or urging a course of action'.

Posters are generally used for conveying a specific message, teaching a particular thing, giving a general idea, etc. Posters exert great influence on the observer

Guidelines for preparing and using a poster

- Promote one point at a time.
- Support local demonstrations and exhibits.
- It should be planned for specified people on a specified topic and a theme should be provided.
- It should have instant appeal.
- It should tell the message in a single glance.

• It should be attractive enough and pleasing colours should be used.

• For headings, bold letters (20 × 30 inch) should be used.

• The language should be easy and simple.

• The most suitable words should be decided upon to provide a title or a slogan.

• A few layouts should be sketched and the best one should be decided on.

• All needed material should be gathered to prepare the poster.

• Smudge marks should be erased and finishing touches added.

• The poster must be displayed at a place with good provision of light and where a large number of people can see it.

Advantages of a poster

• Because of its impressive presentation, a poster captivates the eye, regardless of the message and is capable of being comprehended. • A poster is a simple and dynamic medium of presenting a message in a compact form. • A poster tells the story vividly with the desired effect.

Limitations of a poster

• A poster conveys a single theme and does not always give enough information. • The lettering if not attractive and accurate makes the poster illegible. • Smudge marks make the posters unattractive and futile.

Q 10 Electronic media

= Electronic media:

Electronic media may include television, film and radio, movies, internet, CDs, DVDs and other devices like cameras and video consoles.

A. Television TV has become the most popular of all media. It is effective in not only creating awareness, but also to an extent influencing public opinion and introducing new ways of life. The importance of the television is given below: • It is a good source of entertainment. • It keeps our knowledge up to date. • Advertisements inform general public about various health programmes and new ideas. • It provides us with latest information. • It contributes positively to the education of the society and provides awareness to the people.

B. B. Radio It is found nearly in every home. In many developing countries, the radio has a broader audience than television as it can also be seen in the remotest of villages. The radio transmission serves as a vital agency of mass education if used effectively as it is also approachable by poor people. Example, the Government is promoting Kangaroo Mother Care for preterm and low birth weight babies through radio these days. Most common advantages of the radio are as follows:

• It can be valuable aid in putting across useful information in the form of straight talks, plays questions and answers and quiz programmes. • It is cheaper and portable. • It is good for mass education.

• Radio programmes with dramatic effects can arouse positive emotions and reinforce positive attitude. • It keeps our knowledge up to date. • It is also a good source of entertainment, news, sports and traffic events. • People can listen to the radio even by closing their eyes as it is only audible.

Q 11 . Blackboard / chalk board. Advantages and disadvantages .

= Chalkboard/blackboard

A blackboard is any dark-coloured, flat, smooth surface on which one can write or draw with a chalk . It is one of the oldest and simplest visual aids.

A chalkboard is also known as a blackboard that is a dark-coloured writing surface especially black or green in colour used for classroom teaching by writing or drawing illustrations using sticks of chalks.

Originally, chalkboards were prepared using smooth, thin sheets of slate or stone of black or dark grey colour. However, in the new era, green coloured blackboards are becoming more popular because of their better compatibility viewers' vision.

Advantages of a chalkboard

• It is simple to use with little practice.

• It is economical and reusable.

• It is easily available and can be used any time.

• It can be used in a wide variety of ways, for simple outlines, drawings, summary of main points, etc.

• It encourages active doing and seeing on the part of the audience.

• It is a natural supplement to all aids and mistakes can be quickly erased.

• It can be easily used for giving lesson notes to students.

Limitations of a chalkboard

• It cannot preserve written material.

• It cannot be used for a large audience.

• It requires imagination, initiation, practice and preparation.

• It interrupts communication.

• It becomes smooth and full of glare when used constantly.

• It makes students heavily dependent on the teacher.

• It makes the teacher paced.

• It makes the lesson a dull routine.

• It makes the chalk powder spread, which can be inhaled by the teacher and students.

Q 12 Purposes of a Blackboard / chalk board.

= **Purposes of a chalkboard**

The main purposes of the blackboard are as follows:

• It makes group instruction more concrete and understandable.

• It can set standards of neatness, accuracy and speed, if used properly.

• It can restore the attention of the group.

• It helps in avoiding many vague statements that can be clarified by drawing sketches, outlines, diagrams, directions and summaries.

• It initiates aural and visual sensations and helps in learning.

• It can be a means of motivation and interest.

• It can be used for recording the progress and status.

• It provides many educational opportunities in all curricular and cocurricular activities. The teacher can present facts, principles, processes, procedures, assign individual responsibilities, write questions, problems, sources and references, summaries, outlines, directions, practice individual drills or creative work, make graphic demonstrations, screen for still pictures, projections, symbolic representations and review the total lesson and announcements.

• It can be used to state questions, cite examples of work desired, pose problems and list sources for study.

• It helps in illustrating forms of charting and providing opportunity for nursing students to practice charting.

• It helps in clarifying abstract statements at the exposition stage and providing a summary containing the salient features at recapitulation stage. • It provides a lot of scope for creative and decorative work.

• It helps in starting afresh by erasing writings and drawings.

Q 13 Purposes of Bulletin board

= A bulletin board is a display board that shows the visual learning material on a specific subject. It is a soft board that holds pins or tags. It is a simple device placed either indoors or outdoors.

Items like photographs, publications, posters, newspaper cut-outs are generally displayed

Purposes of bulletin boards Bulletin boards are used for the following purposes:

• Communication of ideas

• Giving correct initial impression

• Broaden the sensory experience

- Intensify impressions
- Vitalize instructions
- Add variety to classroom activity
- Provide information
- Supplement and correlate instructions
- Save time
- Help students learn how to communicate ideas visually
- Facilitate class study of single copy material
- Encourage participation
- Provide a review

Q 14. Explain Objective structured clinical examination (OSCE)

= Objective structured clinical examination (OSCE) is a modern type of examination often used in health sciences (e.g. medicine, dentistry nursing, pharmacy and physiotherapy) to assess clinical skill performance and competence in skills such as communication, clinical examination, medical and nursing procedures/prescription, exercise prescription, joint mobilization/manipulation techniques and interpretation of results.

I. Definitions of OSCE

Objective Structured Clinical Examination (OSCE) is a form of performance-based testing used to measure candidates' clinical competence. During an OSCE, candidates are observed and evaluated as they go through a series of stations in which they interview, examine and treat standardized patients who present with some type of medical problem.

The OSCE is an approach to the assessment of clinical competence in which the components of competence are assessed in a planned or structured way with attention being paid to the objectivity of the examination.

II. Uses of OSCE

OSCE can be used for undergraduate as well as postgraduate nursing students to assess their clinical competencies.

Generally, ranges of basic and advanced clinical practice skills are assessed by using a 10-station OSCE session which comprises practice stations such as physical examination stations, history-taking stations, stations that cover communication skills and stations to perform nursing procedures followed by response stations to ask related multiple choice or short answer questions.

Generally, the following range of practical skills are typically assessed in nursing using OSCE:

- Interpersonal and communication skills
- History-taking skills
- Physical examination of specific body systems
- Mental health assessment
- Clinical decision making, including the formation of differential diagnosis
- Clinical problem-solving skills
- Interpretation of clinical findings and investigations
- Management of a clinical situation, including treatment and referral
- Patient education
- Health promotion
- Acting safely and appropriately in an urgent clinical situation
- Basic and advanced nursing care procedure practices.

III. Organizing the OSCE

- The OSCE examination consists of about 10–15 stations, each of which requires about 4–5 minutes. The number of stations and time spent on each station may vary based on needs of evaluation.
- All stations should be capable of being completed in the same time.
- The students are rotated through all stations and have to move to the next station at the signal.
- As the stations are generally independent, students can start at any procedure stations and complete the cycle.
- Thus, using 15 stations of 4 minutes each, 15 students can complete the examination within 1 hour.

• Each station is designed to test a component of clinical competence.

• At some stations, called the procedure stations, students are given tasks to perform on patients or simulators (some of the essential examples of procedure stations that may be used for first year B.Sc. Nursing students are).

At all such stations there are observers with agreed upon checklists or rating scales to score the student's performance

Q 15. Functions of poster

= Posters are used to:

• Present a single idea or subject forcefully.

• Communicate a more general idea.

• Publicize important school and community events and projects.

• Thrust the message leading to action for the classroom and community.

• Add atmosphere to the classroom.

• Capture attention by some attractive feature and thus convey the message attractively and quickly.

• Motivate the learners in the class

• Leave a strong lasting impression on the learner's mind.

• Satisfy the viewer emotionally and aesthetically and to create atmospheric effect.

CHAPTER EIGHT

ASSESSMENT

SHORT ANSWER QUESTIONS

Q 1. Advantages & Disadvantages of multiple choice questions.

= Multiple-choice questions (MCQs) are the form of assessment where respondents are asked to select the best possible answer (or answers) out of choices from a list.

MCQs are a special type of questions that are widely used in various entrance exams where thousands of students attempt the exams. These are standardized tests with high reliability and validity.

Advantages of MCQs

- Easy to use and administer.
- Can cover a large content area of syllabus.
- Easy to check answers.
- High reliability and validity.
- No scope of subjective biasness.
- Allow more adequate sampling of content.
- Tend to more effectively structure the problem to be addressed.
- Questions can be used more efficiently and reliably than just supplying items.

• Different response alternatives can provide diagnostic feedback about the planned questions (item analysis is possible).

• Questions can be constructed to address various levels of cognitive complexities.

Disadvantages of MCQs

• Not useful to test the highest level of cognitive domain.

• Difficult to construct good MCQs.

• Provide an opportunity to guess the answer if the question is not properly constructed.

• More suitable format for cheating in students if the invigilator is not highly keen in observing students.

• A time-consuming process to construct good questions.

• Can lead the instructor to favour simple recall of facts.

• High degree of dependence on student's readings and instructor's writing ability.

• Measuring synthesis and evaluation can be difficult.

• Inappropriate for measuring the outcomes that require skilled performance.

Q 2 . Constructing multiple choice questions.

= **Guidelines to construct good MCQs**

The following basic rules must be observed for writing good multiple-choice questions :

A . General tips

• Design each item to measure an important learning objective or learning outcome.

• Before writing a question, think about what it is that you want to test. Lecture notes, textbook readings, assigned problems and other course materials can be an inspiration to write items.

• Control the difficulty of the item either by varying the problem in the stem or by changing the alternatives.

• Make certain that each item is independent of the other items in the test.

• Make sure that each item is grammatically accurate to avoid ambiguity in understanding.

• Keep the question stem and alternatives as short as possible. Use few words. Avoid repeating words from the question stem in the alternatives.

• Make sure to have a sufficient number of easy and more challenging questions so that the poor, fair, good and excellent students are effectively judged and separated.

• Try to make the first few MCQs relatively quick and easy, to help calm students down so they can focus on the more challenging questions to come.

• Avoid the temptation to test many things in one question. If possible, try to write more than one MCQ rather than test multiple concepts in one question.

• Ask more than one questions when a fair amount of information must be provided as it takes time for students to carefully read and understand the information you provide in a test. For example, you could give them a table of results, a graph, or a scenario and then ask two or three different MCQs about it.

• Do not try to write the entire test in one day; it takes time, creativity and thought to write good MCQs.

• After constructing the MCQ test, a try-out may be planned on nearly similar subjects and an item analysis must be carried out before preparation of a final draft of the test. B. Construction of the stem

• Present a single, clearly formulated problem in the stem of the item/question.

• Phrase the question stem as clearly and concisely as possible, avoiding complex language.

• State the stem of the item in a positive form, wherever possible.

• Emphasize negative wording whenever it is used in the stem of an item; for example, which of the following is NOT an appropriate method of back massage?

• Avoid verbal clues, which might enable students to select the correct answer or to eliminate an incorrect alternative. Similarity of wording in both the stem and the correct answer is one of the more obvious clues.

C. Construction of alternatives

• Make certain that the intended answer is correct or clearly the best.

• Make all alternatives grammatically consistent with the stem of the item and parallel in form.

• Avoid the use of the alternative 'all of the above' and use 'none of the above' with great caution.

• Do not include alternatives such as 'both (A) and (D)' or 'all but (C)', as these complicate the structure of the question and tend to confuse students and/or slow them down.

• Vary the position of the correct answer in a random manner.

• Vary the relative length of the correct answer to eliminate length as a clue.

• There is no set rule about the number of options you should include in MCQs. The greater the number of options, the smaller the mathematical chance of correct guesswork. Therefore, generally 4–5 alternatives are used.

• Make the distracters plausible and attractive to the uninformed, by:

• Using common misconceptions or common errors of students as distracters.

• Using good sounding words (e.g. accurate, important, etc.) in the distracters, as well as in the correct answers.

• Making the distracters similar to the correct answer in both length and complexity of wording.

• Stating the alternatives in the language of the student.

• Construct the destructors as close as possible to the correct answer to make most effective destructors.

Q 3. Advantages & Disadvantages of objective type questions.

= Objective examination can be part of formative (diagnostic) and summative (final assessment) exams. Most popular objective exam is Multiple Choice Questions (MCQ)

=

Advantages	Disadvantages
• It is easy to apply and score. • All kinds of information can be measured. • To answer the question takes a short time. • It is suitable to be used in exams for groups with high participation. • It is easily applicable at all levels and stages of education. • Reliability and content validity are high since it is possible to ask many questions in the exam. • When the answers are not marked on the exam paper, the exam paper can be used repeatedly. • The exam results are objective since they do not vary from evaluator to evaluator. • It provides a variety of statistical applications. Statistical procedures can be carried out with data obtained from the exam.	• There is a chance success. • It does not improve the ability of expression. • Most of the test time is spent on reading choices and finding the right answer. • It measures knowledge and remembering and is limited in measuring information that is at the level of synthesis and evaluation. • The forming, organizing, and writing of the questions requires expertise and experience. • It is not used much in the measurement of advanced behaviors.

Q 4. Define evaluation. Discuss the purposes of evaluation

= Evaluation is the process of determining to what extent the educational objectives are being realized. —Ralph Tyler

Evaluation is the process of determining the extent to which objectives are being achieved, the effectiveness of the learning experiences provided in the classroom and how well the goals of education have been accomplished. —NCERT

Evaluation is the assessment of merits and or worth. —Scriven

Evaluation is a value judgment on an observation, 'performance test' or indeed any data whether directly measured or inferred. —International Dictionary of Education

Evaluation is a systematic examination of educational and social progress. —Conbach et al

Purposes of assessment/evaluation

Evaluation serves distinct purposes for students, teachers, curriculum and society. The teacher should have a complete programme of evaluation, which should be considered an integral, continuous part of teaching as it enables the teacher to accomplish essential purposes.

Evaluation serves the following distinct purposes for students, teachers, curriculum and society:

- To provide short-term goals to the students to work towards the achievement of educational objectives.
- To clarify the intended learning outcome.
- To determine the level of knowledge and understanding in students.
- To diagnose the strengths and weaknesses of students.
- To encourage student learning by measuring their achievement and informing them about their success.
- To provide information to students for overcoming learning difficulties and selecting future learning experiences.
- To estimate the effectiveness of the instructional media used and the usefulness of instructional materials.
- To help students acquire the attitude and skills of self-evaluation.
- To assess the nonscholastic domains of the student's personality (interests, attitudes and values).
- To provide feedback to the students about their strengths and weaknesses requiring their special attention.
- To assess the student's progress throughout the year.
- To determine whether a particular student is competent enough to be advanced to the next class.
- To ascertain if the teaching strategies are effective and if there is a need to change the teaching strategies.
- To improve curriculum in light of recent advances.
- To satisfy the university requirements for a curriculum.
- To recommend the names of students eligible for a degree to the university.
- To report the student's progress to parents.

• To prevent the society from quacks and incompetent professionals by blocking them from getting degrees/diplomas.

• Evaluation is carried out for general and educational research.

Q 6 Write the observation checklist for the first year B.Sc. nursing student for procedure .

=

Patient's Name: ______________________ IP No.: ______________________
Ward: ______________________

Checklist	Yes	No	Remarks
Preparation of patient and unit			
Explain the procedure to the patient			
Remove unnecessary items from the work area and place the articles needed conveniently on the bedside table			
Bring the patient to the edge of the bed and toward the nurse to prevent overreaching			
Check the room temperature and warm it if necessary			
Close the windows, if necessary and put off the fan to prevent draughts			
Provide privacy by means of curtains			
Remove the top bed linen or fanfold them to the foot end of the bed, leaving a sheet or bath blanket over the patient; keep it free at the foot end, to allow freedom for the legs			
Keep patient prone or on side according to the patient's condition.			
Remove the personal clothing and cover patient with the bath blanket			
Procedure			
Wash hands			
Mix hot and cold water in the basin and check the temperature on the back of the hand. Fill the basin half or full			
Assist the patient to turn to a prone or side-lying position Position the bath blanket and towel to expose only the back till buttocks with the face away from the nurse; make sure that the patient will not fall			
Fold back the bath blanket from the shoulder to the thighs and tuck the edges secularly around the thighs; place the towel over the bed, close to the back, lengthwise			
Wash, rinse and dry the patient's back from the shoulders to the buttocks with brisk circular movements			
After drying the back give a thorough back rub with methylated spirit and powder			
Pay particular attention to the pressure points and cleansing between gluteal folds			
Observe for any indication of redness or skin breakdown in the sacral area and bony prominences			
Put on the clean gown/patient clothes			
Wash hands			

Q 7. Difference between formative evaluation and summative evaluation. / List the types of evaluation.

= Types of assessment/evaluation

The description of the types of assessment or evaluation

Parameters	Formative assessment	Summative assessment
Meaning	It is an ongoing assessment of the student's achievement while the instructional course/ programme is in progress.	It is the final assessment of the student's achievement at the end of a unit/course/ programme.
Purposes	To monitor the progress of students and provide feedback for improvement while instructions are in progress.	To finally assign the grades or pass/fail status in a particular educational module or programme.
Frequency	Carried out quite frequently ranging from daily to weekly while instructions are in progress.	Carried out monthly, biannually, annually or at the end of a semester course/progress.
Content focus	Detailed focus on content.	General and broad content scope.
Methods	Methods of formative assessment include classroom questioning, daily assignments, regular formal/informal observation, class tests and internal assessments.	Methods of summative assessment include project evaluation, term examination and final external examination.

CHAPTER NINE

INFORMATION, EDUCATION & COMMUNICATION

SHORT ANSWER QUESTIONS

Q 1. Approaches / Aims in health education.

= Aims of health education

The definition adopted by WHO in 1969 and the Alma Ata declaration adopted in 1978 provide a useful basis for formulating the aims and objectives of health education.

These are as follows:

- To help the people understand that health is the most valuable community asset, and to help them achieve optimum health by their own activities and efforts.
- To develop a sense of responsibility for improving their health as individual members of families and communities.
- To develop scientific knowledge, attitude, skills on health matters to enable people to develop correct habits.
- To educate people for proper use of health services in whatever forms it is made available to them by the government.

• To alter behaviour that may have directly or indirectly influenced the occurrence or spread of diseases in a given setting, a culturally relevant health education programme can be planned only after understanding the behaviour in all its manifestations.

• To promote the greater possible fulfilment of inherited powers of the body and the mind and happy adjustment of an individual in the society.

• To provide a person with appropriate knowledge to enjoy decent health and also knowledge about the occurrence and spread of disease thus enabling him to adopt relevant preventive measures.

• To create in him an interest in his own health and well-being.

• To create in him an interest for the health of other members of his family as well those living in his surroundings.

• To create in him a desire to support health education programmes in his area. In a nutshell, the focus of health education is on people and action. Its goal is to make realistic improvements in the basic quality of life.

Q 2. Principles of health education.

= **Principles of health education**

Health education encompasses two activities: teaching and learning. Teaching is ineffective without learning. Both the health educator and the patient are responsible for bringing about a change in health knowledge, health attitude and behaviour. Some essential principles of health education are discussed below

• **Credibility of message:**

It is the degree to which the message to be communicated is perceived as trustworthy by the receiver.

• **Creating interest among participants:**

It is a psychological principle that people are unlikely to listen to things that are not of their interest. If a health programme is based on the felt needs, people will participate in the programme willingly.

• **Motivating the participants:**

Motivation is like a petrol engine that drives the mental engine. It is the fundamental desire in every person to learn. Motivation is contagious; one motivated person may spread motivation throughout the group.

• **Enhance comprehension of content:**

It means health education should be based on the level of understanding, education and literacy of people at whom the teaching is directed. Teaching should be within the mental capacity of the audience.

• **Ensure reinforcement:**

Repetition at intervals is necessary to promote learning. Without reinforcement and feedback, students can go back to the preawareness stage.

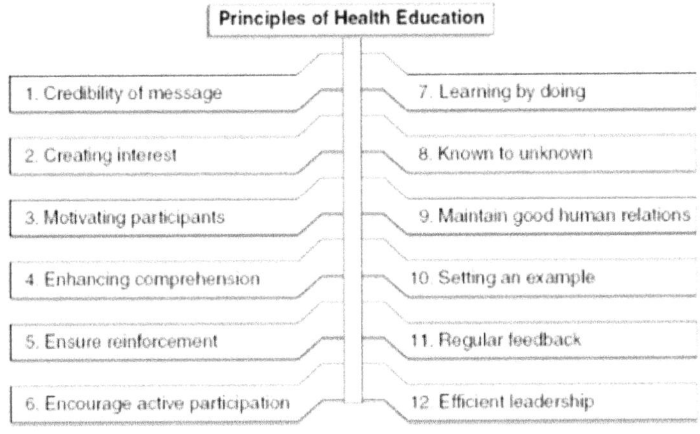

Principles of health education.

• **Encourage active participation:**

Participation is a key word in health education. It is based on the psychological principle of learning. Health education should aim at encouraging people to work actively with health workers and others in identifying their own health problems and also in developing solutions. The Alma Ata declaration states, 'the people have a right and duty to participate individually and collectively in the planning and implementation of their health care'.

- **Learning by doing: Teaching is effective when individuals actively** participate in health education. Learning becomes active and quicker if the individuals are made active physically as well as psychologically.
- **Known to unknown: It is based on the appreciative mass theory of** learning. The people in a community know something and the health educator enlarges this knowledge. If the health educator links new knowledge with the old knowledge, it can enhance learning.
- **Maintaining good human relations: Sharing of information, ideas and** feelings happens most easily between people who have a good relationship.
- **Setting an example: The health educators should set a good example** in the topic they are dealing with as it fosters better understanding.

Regular feedback:

Feedback is one of the key concepts of the system approach. The health educator can modify the elements of the system in light of the feedback from his audience. For effective communication, feedback is of paramount importance.

- **Efficient leadership: Leaders are agents of change and they can be** made use of in health education work. Psychologists have shown and established that we learn best from people we respect and regard.

The essential attributes of a leader are as follows:

- Understands the needs of the community.
- Provides proper guidance.
- Takes initiative.
- Is receptive to the views and suggestions of people.
- Identifies himself with the community.
- Is selfless, honest, impartial, considerate and sincere.

• Is easily accessible to people.

Q 6 Explain in detail about mass media .

= Definitions of mass media

It is defined as a one-way communication that is useful in transmitting messages to the people even in the remotest places.

Mass media is those means of communication that reach and influence large numbers of people, especially newspapers, popular magazines, radio and television. Mass media are those media that are created to be consumed by large number of people worldwide and also a direct contemporary instrument of mass communication.

Classification of mass media

Mass media may be classified as follows:

• Electronic media: Electronic media may include television, film and radio, movies, internet, CDs, DVDs and other devices like cameras and video consoles.

• Performing media: This includes music, songs, dramas, skits, puppet shows, poetry, speech, gossip and jokes.

• Visual media: Paintings, handicrafts, costumes, certain printed literature such as books, pamphlets, leaflets, brochures, newsletters, journals, magazines and newspaper make up the visual media.

Methods of mass media communication

The common methods used for mass media communication are television, film and radio, movies, internet, CDs, DVDs and other devices like cameras and video consoles. Alternatively, print media use a physical object such as newspapers, magazines, brochures, newsletters, books, leaflets and pamphlets as a means of sending their information.

A. Television TV has become the most popular of all media. It is effective in not only creating awareness, but also to an extent influencing public opinion and introducing new ways of life. The importance of the television is given below: • It is a good source of entertainment. • It keeps our knowledge up to date. • Advertisements inform general public about various health programmes and new ideas. • It provides us with latest information. • It contributes positively to the education of the society and provides awareness to the people.

B. Radio

It is found nearly in every home. In many developing countries, the radio has a broader audience than television as it can also be seen in the remotest of villages. The radio transmission serves as a vital agency of mass education if used effectively as it is also approachable by poor people. Example, the Government is promoting Kangaroo Mother Care for preterm and low birth weight babies through radio these days.

C. Newspapers

The newspaper today plays a vital role in human affairs.

The importance of newspapers is as follows:

• They play an important part both in the national and international areas. They give us news and views. The way a man wants food for his belly, he also needs news for his mind to keep pace with the world.

• They refresh our knowledge and ideas.

• They broaden our outlook and change views.

• They educate the common people.

• They shape the opinions of the common people of a country by influencing public opinion. ..

Author Information

Name : Rutwik Upendra Bhalshankar.

Email : rutwik61@gmail.com

Mobile No : 9130024431

Books Available on : Amazon , Flipkart, Notionpress

www.ingramcontent.com/pod-product-compliance
Ingram Content Group UK Ltd.
Pitfield, Milton Keynes, MK11 3LW, UK
UKHW021659190726
13853UKWH00001B/365

9 798888 055670